ADVENTURE G

Ghost Train

Stephen Thraves

Illustrated by Peter Dennis

HODDER AND STOUGHTON
LONDON SYDNEY AUCKLAND

British Library Cataloguing in Publication Data

Thraves, Stephen
  Ghost train.
  1. Fantasy role-playing games
  I. Title II. Dennis, Peter *1950-* III. Series
  793.93

  ISBN 0-340-54308-6

Text copyright © Stephen Thraves 1991
Illustrations copyright © Peter Dennis 1991

First published 1991
Second impression 1992

All rights reserved. No part of this publication may be reproduced or transmitted in any form or by any means, electronically or mechanically, including photocopying, recording, or any information storage and retrieval system, without either prior permission in writing from the publisher or a licence permitting restricted copying. In the United Kingdom such licences are issued by the Copyright Licensing Agency, 90 Tottenham Court Road, London W1P 9HE.

The rights of Stephen Thraves to be identified as the author of the text of this work and of Peter Dennis to be identified as the illustrator of this work have been asserted by them in accordance with the Copyright, Designs and Patents Act 1988.

Published by Hodder and Stoughton Children's Books,
a division of Hodder and Stoughton Ltd,
Mill Road, Dunton Green, Sevenoaks, Kent TN13 2YA

Photoset by Rowland Phototypesetting Ltd,
Bury St Edmunds, Suffolk

Printed in Great Britain by BPCC Hazell Books,
BPCC Hazells Ltd
Member of BPCC Ltd

Have you ever seen a GHOST TRAIN? In a remote part of the Scottish Highlands some farmers claim they have. They say on a stormy night you can sometimes see its eerie glow speeding through the glen! Or you can hear its haunting whistle echoing round the mountains . . .

They insist it's the eight-thirty from Inverness which used to travel along this now abandoned and dilapidated stretch of track some ninety years ago. There was a terrible storm one night, and high winds buckled a bridge which carried the line over a wide, deep river. The train and all its passengers plunged to their doom!

Some might say that it was as much as those passengers deserved for they were a gang of thieves who had hijacked the train a few miles further up the line. There was a shipment of gold on board and they intended to divert it along a rarely-used side track. But the ill-fated bridge was as far as they got.

Strangely, although the submerged wreckage was searched from end to end by divers, the three large chests of gold were nowhere to be found. One theory is that the hijackers, worried about the safety of the bridge, stopped the train a short distance before. To lighten their load, they removed the chests and hid them somewhere at the edge of the railway line. They intended to come back for them at a later date . . . but that was not to be, of course!

Unfortunately, no one has ever dared to test this theory. The terrified locals keep well away from the desolate track. How about you, though? Are you brave enough to search for that gold?

You will not necessarily discover the gold on your first exploration. It may well take several goes. Keep trying, though, and you will eventually be successful. And remember that there are *three* crates of gold to be found in all. So when you have uncovered one crate, you may well want to try further explorations for the others. You'll find that there are many different routes you can take in your search – each route involving different clues and adventures.

So the game can be played over and over – as many times as your nerves can stand it!

PREPARATION FOR YOUR VISIT

Well, you're certainly not going to explore this spooky-sounding railway line on your own. You might be brave – but not that brave! So you decide to get in touch with your two friends; Professor Bones, the celebrated 'ghostologist', and Miss Harriet Crumble, the famous medium. They both accompanied you on a previous ghost-exploration to Oastley Towers, the eerie mansion known to the local residents as Ghostly Towers.

To be honest, they had proved rather disappointing companions. Although they both claimed to be used to ghosts, they were just as nervous inside Ghostly Towers as you were. In fact, you were convinced neither of them had ever seen a ghost before! Still, you go and pay them both a visit . . .

Thin, absent-minded Professor Bones says he would be delighted to accompany you on your trip, quickly rooting out his special ghost-hunter's knapsack. You can't help noticing, however, the nervous little blinks behind his spectacles. He's obviously thinking about the last occasion he agreed to join you. But he's presumably worried about his reputation if he refuses! You suspect the same of Miss Crumble. The excited beam on her plump face seems a slightly false one. Her little Scottish terrier, Spooks, makes no such pretence. He also joined your exploration to Ghostly Towers and he doesn't mind anyone knowing that it was the most terrifying experience of his short life! But a dog is a dog and if his eccentric mistress orders him to come on a ghost hunt, what choice does he have? It's just not fair, somehow . . .

So your little band immediately travels up to Scotland on the overnight express, Miss Crumble telling you that she has again brought her *special dice* with her. This is a sort of portable crystal ball to help her make important decisions. You leave the train at Inverness and take a local bus to the tiny village of Coldhaggis. This is about five miles away from the haunted stretch of railway line – and the nearest anyone dares live! There's a small museum in the village commemorating the disaster and you have a chat with its timid curator, Mr Sporran.

He strongly advises you against exploring the railway line, saying no one has done so for the last twenty years. And that person ended up going stark raving mad! When he sees that you are determined, however, he says that some of the items in the museum might be of help in your exploration. He shows you an old map of the railway line and two large rusty keys (one green, one orange) which used to give access to the various little buildings along the track: the signal box, station, labourers' hut, etc. He also shows you an old notebook discovered near the line just after the disaster, containing a series of strange symbols and instructions. This is believed to be some sort of codebook used by the hijackers when they hid the gold.

Professor Bones eagerly opens his little knapsack so you can take away all these items but Mr Sporran says you can only borrow *one* of them, otherwise he would get into trouble with the owners of the museum. Although you promise to bring them all back again, he is quite adamant. He's obviously not too confident that you will make it back!

That's all the preparation complete. You're now ready to begin your adventure . . .

WHAT TO DO

Your terrifying exploration of the haunted railway line starts at PARAGRAPH ONE. At the end of that paragraph, you will be instructed to go to another paragraph. You keep following these instructions until – hopefully – you uncover the gold.

Quite often during the exploration, you will need one of the ITEMS shown to you by Mr Sporran – those were the map of the railway line, the green key, the orange key, and the hijackers' codebook. These ITEMS accompany this book but don't forget that Mr Sporran will allow you to take only *one* of them. So decide which of the four ITEMS is likely to be the most useful. Be very careful in making this choice because some ITEMS offer you a better chance of completing the adventure than others. Place the ITEM you have chosen into the Professor's little knapsack. You do this by inserting it into the slit of the KNAPSACK CARD.

You may well discover other ITEMS during your exploration of the railway line. If you do, these can be added to the one you set out with – and so, when instructed, place these extra ITEMS into the slit of the KNAPSACK CARD as well. The purpose of this card is to tell you exactly which ITEMS you have for use at any one time (so, after an ITEM has helped at a particular paragraph, always remember to return it to the KNAPSACK CARD). Any ITEM not contained in this card **cannot be used or consulted** – and therefore should be kept out of play.

Of course, I must point out that there's more than a fair chance of seeing ghosts during your exploration of the railway line. I don't like having to say this, but I feel it's only right to warn you. And they're also rather mean ghosts, tending to appear on those occasions when you've just found that you don't have the appropriate ITEM with you.

If you *do* see a ghost, you must – as soon as you've recovered from the shock – record it on the GHOST COUNTER included in the wallet. This is a special invention of Professor Bones for adding up hauntings. You begin your adventure with the GHOST COUNTER set at **zero** – so rotate the disc until **0** appears in the window. Every time you experience a 'haunting', you turn the disc **clockwise** until the next number appears. Your nerves can stand one haunting . . . two . . . even three, but when the GHOST COUNTER shows you've had *four* hauntings, you must immediately leave the railway line, stopping the game there. Of course, you can always make another exploration (perhaps setting out with a different ITEM this time to see if it gives you more luck) but you can only do this by starting at **paragraph one** again.

I'm not sure how wise you are in visiting the eerie railway line but if you must continue, turn the page. And I wish you luck! I've a horrible feeling you might need it . . .

1

After an arduous two hour hike through desolate mountains, you suddenly spot a spine-chilling sight ahead. With a thick grey mist weaving between its girders, it's the faint outline of the collapsed railway bridge! You can just make out its ugly jagged end jutting out into empty space. As you walk a little nearer, you can hear the loose girders eerily creak and groan in the wind. Spooks is petrified and lets out a long, nervous whine! 'Well, if ever a bridge looked likely to be haunted, I'd say *that* one was!' the Professor remarks faintly, reluctant to go any closer. 'Those poor souls. I know they were crooks – but what a terrible fate! I suppose we must walk right up to the bridge.' You sombrely nod your head at the Professor. Yes, your little group *must* – the gold might be hidden only a few metres away from it. But who is to lead you all towards this eerie, mist-shrouded structure? Miss Crumble suggests letting her special dice decide and anxiously takes it from her pocket.

Throw the SPECIAL DICE – then turn to the appropriate paragraph number.

If 💀 thrown   go to 192

If 🦇 thrown   go to 229

If 👻 thrown   go to 67

2

You all eagerly throw back the lid of the iron box and stare inside. Instead of gleaming gold bars, however, there are just rusty hammers and crowbars! 'These were obviously the track-workers' tools,' you remark disappointedly, about to let the lid fall shut again. But the Professor suddenly stops you for his eager, beady eyes have spotted a folded sheet of paper tucked under one of the hammers. 'It's another map of the railway,' he says excitedly, using his sleeve to wipe off the cobwebs. 'This must have belonged to those workmen too!'

If you don't already have it there, put the MAP into the slit of the KNAPSACK CARD. Now go to 168.

3

'Oh, well done, Miss Crumble!' the Professor exclaims in his shrill voice. 'It looks as if we have found the gold already. And without encountering a single ghost!' When you all try to open the iron chest, however, you find that it is well and truly locked. In the midst of everyone's disappointment, the Professor suddenly has an idea. 'If the chest is railway property,' he remarks, 'then maybe it can be unlocked by one of those two keys Mr Sporran showed us!'

Do you have either of the KEYS in the KNAPSACK CARD? If

you do, place it exactly over the chest's 'lock' below to see if it works – then follow the instruction. If you don't have either of the KEYS – or your KEY doesn't work – go to 31 instead.

4

The coded message obviously *had* been chiselled by one of the hijackers! For it works out as: *GOLD HIDDEN WITHIN THREE MILES OF THIS SIGNAL BOX*. 'Well, it's not as helpful as it might have been,' the Professor remarks, tugging his beard thoughtfully as he returns the codebook to his knapsack. 'Three miles is quite a large area. But at least it implies that the gold isn't here. So we needn't search the signal box after all!' As you all leave the eerie-looking building, it's difficult to say who seems the most relieved – the Professor, Miss Crumble or yourself! **Go to 19.**

5

'I'm afraid the fates have decided that you should lead the way to the signal box, Professor,' Miss Crumble tells him sympathetically. He peers down at the symbol showing on her special dice, trying to work out how on earth she had deduced that. But it's obviously a total mystery to him – for he looks very confused as he scratches his bald head! Nevertheless, he accepts Miss Crumble's announcement, gingerly walking to the front of your little group. About half-way to the eerie wooden hut, however, his courage suddenly fails him. 'I'd be interested to see where this signal box is on Mr Sporran's map,' he says, quickly thinking of an excuse for stopping. 'It will show us exactly where we are!'

Use the MAP to find which square the old signal box is in – then follow the appropriate instruction. If you don't have a MAP in the KNAPSACK CARD, you'll have to guess which instruction to follow.

> If you think D2 go to 147
> If you think C2 go to 119
> If you think C1 go to 241

When you have recovered from this haunting, record it on the GHOST COUNTER. Now go to 265.

7

Unfortunately, of course, you didn't borrow the codebook from Mr Sporran. But the Professor says he might be able to decipher the message on the scrap of paper without it. 'Now let me have a look at it,' he hums, twiddling his little moustache. 'It's simply a matter of working out which are the verbs and which are the prepositions. The rest should then be quite obvious.' You can't believe it's quite as easy as that, though, and sure enough, the Professor is still scratching his head over it some five minutes later! 'Just give me a bit longer,' he insists. But you're all suddenly distracted by an eerie hooting sound, echoing round the mountains. You all wonder in panic if the ghost train is about to appear! ***Go to 149.***

8

You are becoming as forgetful as the Professor . . . you don't have the map with you, of course. No wonder Miss Crumble is sighing at you. But is this the real reason for her sighing? For the sigh becomes a long, chant-like one, as if she's suddenly gone into one of her trances. She now starts to speak. 'There's been murder at this castle,' she moans, eerily swaying her head. 'Many centuries ago. A servant stabbed his master in that tall tower up there!' You're sure this is just Miss Crumble's vivid imagination again, but, just in case there's something in it, you suggest quickly leaving the castle. You haven't put it far behind you, however, when you hear a strange wailing noise coming from that direction. Is this the ghost of that stabbed master? You all slowly and anxiously turn your heads . . . ***Go to 92.***

9

You now start your search of the cottage, agreeing to complete it as quickly as possible. Dark, gloomy and strewn with cobwebs, the place quite gives you the shivers! And you keep thinking of what Mr Sporran told you about the farmers who lived near the railway line. Most of them went stark staring mad! Miss Crumble leads you all into what was once obviously the kitchen. Half-hidden under cobwebs, there's an ancient stove and a small chipped sink. Spiders crawl round the plug-hole! 'This must have been the crofter's larder,' Miss Crumble remarks as she tugs at a long door in the corner of the kitchen. 'Well, bless me,' she adds with surprise, 'it's locked!'

Do you have either of the KEYS in the KNAPSACK CARD? If you do, place it exactly over the larder's 'lock' below to see if it works – then follow the instruction. If you don't have either of the KEYS – or your KEY doesn't work – go to 206 instead.

10

Miss Crumble is also of the view that you shouldn't go back to the tunnel. 'If there had been the tiniest bit of gold in there,' she says rather pompously, 'I'm sure I would have sensed it. Perhaps my beads would have started to rattle or my earrings jangle. And if *I* hadn't sensed it, then Spooks would have done. He sometimes gets these sensations as well, you know. His ears cock up or his tongue suddenly hangs out.' You and the Professor glance down at Miss Crumble's little dog, rather sceptical about this. You're wondering if he just does these things to humour his mistress. But his face is looking straight ahead, telling nothing! ***Go to 283.***

11

The coded message is deciphered as: *BEWARE OF THIS ROWING BOAT! I HAVE DELIBERATELY DRILLED HOLES IN THE BOTTOM TO DROWN ANYONE SNIFFING ROUND FOR OUR GOLD. THE GREAT JOKE OF IT IS THAT IT'S NOT IN THE LAKE ANYWAY!* Well, that definitely confirms it. The message *had* been carved by one of the hijackers! 'What an unpleasant bunch they sound,' the Professor remarks with a disapproving sniff as you all continue on your way. 'That coded message was obviously a reminder to themselves when they returned for the gold. And the boat was a deliberate trap for anyone without one of their codebooks!' ***Go to 66.***

12

You now start to follow the disused railway line away from the bridge, wondering where it will take you. But you haven't followed it far when Miss Crumble spots a tiny building through the mist, a couple of hundred metres to the left of the track. 'It looks like a crofter's cottage,' the Professor remarks as he squints through his glasses towards where Miss Crumble is pointing. 'A crofter is the name given to a farmer in these parts – and their cottages usually look just like that one, made of stone with a thatched roof.' ***Go to 293.***

13

Miss Crumble seems to be getting as absent-minded as the Professor. You did *not* borrow the map from the museum but one of the other items. It must be her growing nervousness that made her forget! You wonder *why* Miss Crumble is becoming so nervous. Is it because she's starting to sense something? 'Yes, I'm afraid I am, dear,' she replies tensely when you ask her. 'It's the ghost train. I'm sure it's about to make an appearance!' Just at that moment you see a flash of light in the distance. Was it merely lightning – or sparks from the ghost train's wheels? You all peer into the darkness ahead, waiting for the flash to occur again . . . ***Go to 262.***

14

Once again you have to remind the Professor that you didn't bring the map. 'Oh no, so we didn't!' he hums absent-mindedly. You are all just about to leave the water tank when Miss Crumble's beads start to rattle! You are sure she is secretly causing this herself somehow – just as you're sure she secretly pushes the glass in those seances of hers. But she insists that the rattling has nothing to do with her; it's a sign that a ghost is near! You and the Professor think this is ridiculous but then you suddenly hear a faint whistle from back along the track. Nervously peering into the darkness, you all wonder if this could be the ghost train. *Go to 54.*

15

You *still* can't find your way back to the railway line, searching hopelessly in the mist. In fact you get the awful feeling that you're wandering more and more *away* from it, rather than towards it. 'If only the ghost train would appear right now,' Miss Crumble says hopefully. 'It would at least show us which direction the railway line is in.' That's not a wish that either you or the Professor share, however! You all eventually find yourselves at a large flat boulder and you decide to take a short breather there. Just as the Professor is about to sit down on it, though, he notices that someone has carved out some symbols of a code. Could this have been one of the hijackers?

Use your CODEBOOK CARD to find out what the message says by decoding the instruction below. If you don't have the CODEBOOK CARD in the KNAPSACK CARD, go to 303 instead.

16

As soon as you've opened the church door, you all rush outside. You don't want to hang around in there a second longer than necessary. And you now decide to give the graveyard a miss as well. Miss Crumble makes the excuse that she was never *that* sure that the dice wanted you to explore it anyway! As you all leave the church, continuing on your trek, you ask the Professor if the mysterious locking of that door should officially count as a haunting. 'No, I don't think it should,' he replies thoughtfully. 'Since nothing was seen or heard, it just comes under the category of strange occurrences. A great pity, I know – but we ghostologists do have strict rules about these things!' ***Go to 90.***

17

As your little group continues to follow the river, the Professor starts to have doubts about the route he chose. 'Perhaps it won't lead us back to the railway line after all,' he admits some while later, scratching his domed head. 'I think we'll bear off to the left instead.' So he now leads you away from the river, tramping through the thick bracken. It's not long before you spot a white signpost ahead and you hope that one of the arms will include the direction to the railway line. But when you reach it you find that the signpost is so decayed that all the place names are completely illegible. 'Wait a minute, though, dears,' Miss Crumble remarks just as you're about to move on. 'Look, there's something carved down the side of the post. It seems to be some sort of coded message!'

Use the CODEBOOK CARD to find out what this message says by decoding the instruction below. If you don't have the CODEBOOK in the KNAPSACK CARD, go to 41 instead.

18

After another quarter of an hour or so of walking, you wonder whether you should start making your way back to the railway line. Surely the hijackers wouldn't have carried the gold much further than this? But then a storm suddenly breaks, the sky torn apart by jagged flashes of light. 'We'd better shelter somewhere,' you suggest urgently, realising how exposed you are. The problem is *where?* **Go to 98.**

19

You've followed the railway line for another half-mile or so when you reach an old level-crossing. The rusty gates creak and rattle in the wind. 'Now if I was going to unload a train,' the Professor remarks excitedly, 'this is exactly where I would do it. Don't forget the chests of gold would have been quite heavy. So the hijackers would have wanted the ground to be as firm as possible. Where better than along this farm track that crosses the line? I think we should follow it for a while.' Before you do, however, he suggests looking for the level-crossing on Mr Sporran's map.

Use the MAP to find which square the level-crossing is in – then follow the appropriate instruction. If you don't have the MAP in the KNAPSACK CARD, you'll have to guess which instruction to follow.

> If you think B2   go to 261
> If you think C2   go to 204
> If you think C3   go to 34

20

When you have recovered from this haunting, record it on the GHOST COUNTER. Now go to 205.

21

The Professor's trembling finger draws your attention to the mist-shrouded mountain just to your right. 'Look up there,' he tells you nervously, 'about half-way from the top. There's a huge ghostly figure staring down at us!' But as your own eyes peer up at the 'ghostly figure' you realise that it is not that at all. 'It's just a massive needle of rock, Professor Bones,' you reassure him. And you wonder whether it will be shown on the map.

Use your MAP to find which square the needle of rock is in – then follow the appropriate instruction below. If you don't have the MAP in the KNAPSACK CARD, you'll have to guess which instruction to follow.

If you think B1	go to 153
If you think C1	go to 209
If you think D1	go to 328

22

Having eagerly removed the padlock, you now open the boiler door so you can all look inside. Your faces drop, however, as you see that there's just a thick layer of ash in there! 'Perhaps the gold is hidden underneath!' the Professor says, his face suddenly brightening again. So he puts his long skinny arm through the boiler door, feeling around in the ash. There is a funny little grimace on his face as he does so. It can't be very pleasant for him! But it all seems worthwhile because he suddenly lets out a squeal of delight. You and Miss Crumble are hoping that it's a bar of gold he's touched – but it's just a large orange key!

If you don't already have it there, put the ORANGE KEY into the KNAPSACK CARD. Now go to 46.

23

With excited expectant expressions on your faces, you all help to fling back the lid of the little chest. But your excitement immediately turns to bitter disappointment. For the chest contains only a pair of ladies' shoes, a fur muff and a hat! 'It must have belonged to one of the passengers,' Miss Crumble remarks. 'The poor dear must have left it here when she got off the train at her station. I wonder if I should try and get in touch with her at my next seance to let her know where she left it?' You're just about to point out to Miss Crumble that the chest would hardly be much use to that forgetful lady now when you notice a dusty notebook lying on the carriage floor. It's another copy of the hijackers' codebook!

If you don't already have it there, put the CODEBOOK into the KNAPSACK CARD. Now go to 134.

When you have recovered from this haunting, record it on the GHOST COUNTER. Now go to 18.

25

Since you didn't bring the codebook with you, though, you all try to persuade yourselves that the marks on the ladder aren't that important. 'Well, we can't be *sure* that it was the hijackers who chiselled them there,' Miss Crumble remarks. 'It might just have been one of the engineers who worked in the shed, whiling away his time with a few meaningless doodles!' Your little group now leaves the engine shed . . . and you in fact decide to leave the railway line altogether, quickly making your way back towards Coldhaggis. It's becoming far too dark to continue your exploration – and far too stormy. You'll have to resume your search for the gold some other time, when the conditions are rather less hostile!

If you would like another attempt at finding the hijackers' gold, you must start the game again from the beginning. Try setting off with a different ITEM this time to see if it gives you more luck.

26

'But we didn't *bring* Mr Sporran's map, Professor,' you patiently remind him as he continues to edge forward in front of you. He nervously flashes his torch to the left, then the right. 'Oh, so we didn't!' he remarks tensely. 'What could I have been thinking of!' But you know full well what he was thinking of; the little hut is full of eerie cobwebs and shadows, just the right sort of place for a ghost! 'W-w-what's that?' the Professor stammers as his torch suddenly illuminates something tall and white in the corner. He quickly moves the beam away before you have a chance to see it yourself. 'I'm sure it's nothing, Professor,' you whisper, your throat suddenly becoming dry, as you take the torch from him and nervously direct the beam back to the corner . . . ***Go to 167.***

27

You all venture deeper and deeper into the tunnel, hoping you'll soon reach the other end so you can leave this eerie darkness. But there's still no sign of any light ahead of you – not even the smallest pinprick! You're just wondering whether you should start to head back when Miss Crumble notices a safe in the wall of the tunnel. You can just about see the following inscription on it: *SPARE LAMPS FOR USE IN EMERGENCY. TO OPEN, USE SPECIAL RAILWAY KEY.* 'I wonder if that's one of the keys Mr Sporran showed us,' you say. You're wondering something else as well. Could the gold be hidden inside the safe?

Do you have either of the KEYS in the KNAPSACK CARD? If

you do, place it exactly over the safe's 'lock' below to see if it works – then follow the instruction. *(You may try both KEYS if you have them.)* If you don't have either of the KEYS – or your KEY doesn't work – go to 266 instead.

28

You try the handle again. This time the door *does* let you in. Borrowing the Professor's torch, you cautiously step into the dark interior of the mountain-rescue hut. You notice several coils of climbing rope hanging from the wall and some old stretchers stacked up on the floor. These would have been used to carry down anyone who was injured in the mountains. You wonder if the ghosts of those people still visit the hut. With its eerie silence and thick trailing cobwebs, the place is certainly just right for a ghost. You half expect to spot one at any moment – with a bandage round its head or its arm in a sling! ***Go to 109.***

29

But nothing does appear from the mist . . . and the rumbling sound from the railway line suddenly stops. 'It must just have been a vibration,' the Professor remarks with obvious relief. 'An unstable bridge like this will do a lot of vibrating. Especially when three humans and a dog suddenly walk along it! You see, it's just as I'm always saying. You should always consider the rational explanations first!' The Professor is so pleased with his calm logic that he gives the small chest a gentle kick. It topples over the edge of the bridge, plunging into the dark river way below! This is not quite the disaster it first appears, however. For you notice that the chest has bobbed to the surface of the water. If there *had* been any gold inside, it would surely have sunk! ***Go to 69.***

30

When you have recovered from this haunting, record it on the GHOST COUNTER. Now go to 248.

31

The Professor might well have been right, of course. Perhaps one of those keys shown to you by Mr Sporran *would* have unlocked the chest. But certainly not the item you had chosen! 'I'm sure this chest *doesn't* contain the gold, anyway,' you say, trying to cheer everyone up. 'Just feel the weight of it. Gold would be a lot heavier, surely!' You all start to climb back up the steep bank but half-way up you suddenly hear a strange wailing noise behind you. It's coming from the river! 'You don't think it's the ghost of one of those drowned hijackers, do you?' you ask through chattering teeth. Everyone very slowly turns round to check . . . **Go to 280.**

32

'Before we get too disappointed that we can't unlock this box,' you remark, 'let's see how heavy it is. If we're able to lift it, then there obviously isn't any gold inside anyway!' You all manage to lift the iron box quite easily – so you're not bothered by the lack of the right key after all! You're just lowering the box to the floor again when Miss Crumble suddenly shivers, nearly dropping her corner. 'I can sense a strange atmosphere in this hut,' she announces ominously, 'as if those workmen are still sitting here!' You and Professor Bones dismiss this as Miss Crumble's imagination, but then you hear a rattling sound from the stove behind you. It's one of those tin mugs on the top! Hearts pounding away, you all slowly turn your heads towards the stove. Are the ghosts of those workmen having a quick cup of tea? **Go to 203.**

33

Your little group has now walked a good way further from the stone tower. Just as you're all thinking that you are *never* going to find your way back to the railway line, you trip over something hard and only just manage to recover your balance. But you almost wouldn't have minded if you *had* crashed to the ground for, much to your delight, you notice that it's an iron track that made you trip. At last you've returned to the railway line! ***Go to 107.***

34

You haven't followed the farm track far when it suddenly disappears into a tunnel. 'How strange!' the Professor remarks, scratching his domed head, deep in thought. 'This farm track must have once been a branch line of the railway, but the rails have long since been pulled up – probably even before the hijacking took place. Perhaps the hijackers knew about this old tunnel, though, and carried some of the gold here.' So, although you're all rather reluctant about the idea, it looks as if you're going to have to explore the dark, spooky tunnel. Which poor person is to take the lead? Miss Crumble says it would be fairest if you let her special dice decide . . .

Throw the SPECIAL DICE – then turn to the appropriate number.

If ☠ thrown	go to 224
If 🦇 thrown	go to 282
If 🐔 thrown	go to 199

35

'Well, did you find any gold?' Miss Crumble asks eagerly as you eventually leave the cottage and return to where the others are waiting for you. You shake your head, having to disappoint her. 'But I did come across what looks like a coded message,' you add. 'It was scratched above the little fireplace in the kitchen. I copied it on to this old scrap of paper with a piece of charcoal I found in the grate.'

Use the CODEBOOK CARD to find out what this message says by decoding the instruction below. If you don't have the CODEBOOK in your KNAPSACK CARD, go to 7 instead.

36

As hard as you peer into the mist, however, no ghost dog appears. 'It must have just been the wind howling round the mountains,' the Professor says, relaxing a little. 'What a pity! I've never seen a ghost dog before. It would have been –' But his relieved voice suddenly stops as the eerie barking starts again. It appears to be coming from the chimney! 'Here, doggy,' Miss Crumble says nervously, trying to placate it, but then she starts to frown. 'I'm sure I recognise that bark,' she says and she suddenly marches firmly back into the cottage, making her way to the little kitchen. There is *Spooks*, standing at the fireplace and barking up the chimney. Was he trying to scare you all deliberately so you would go home? You'll never know! **Go to 312.**

37

Having pulled open the larder door, you're all disappointed to see that there are only old tins of food inside. All disappointed except Spooks, that is, because one of the tins has a picture of a happy, healthy dog on it. It's dog food, for the crofter's sheepdog, presumably. 'No, I'm not going to open it for you, Spooks!' Miss Crumble insists as he starts to jump up excitedly. She moves the tin up a couple of shelves, out of Spooks's sight. It's then that you notice something that had been hidden behind it. Lying in the thick dust is a large orange key!

If you don't already have it there, put the ORANGE KEY into the KNAPSACK CARD. Now go to 312.

38

When you have recovered from this haunting, record it on the GHOST COUNTER. Now go to 241.

39

Will your little group *never* find its way back to the railway line? You're still completely lost in the mist, the track nowhere in sight. You could be miles from it by now for all you know. But then Spooks gives a quiet *woof!* . . . then a slightly louder one. 'What is it, my little doggypoos?' Miss Crumble asks him. 'Do you think we're nearing the railway line at last?' Spooks seems to dislike being called 'doggypoos' – or any other silly name his mistress cares to think of for him – but he wags his tail, leading you all towards a large coal-yard. This coal must have been for the steam engines . . . so the railway line must be very near now! For the moment, though, you suggest giving the coal-yard a quick search. Perhaps some of the gold is hidden there! But there's a padlock on the rusty gates to the yard. You're going to need the right key . . .

Do you have either of the KEYS in the KNAPSACK CARD? If you do, place it exactly over the padlock's 'lock' below to see if it works – then follow the instruction. (You may try both KEYS if you have them.) If you don't have either of the KEYS – or your KEY doesn't work – go to 240 instead.

40

But you didn't bring Mr Sporran's map with you, of course. Had the Professor forgotten this, or did he know full well? Either way, you just have to accept his opinion about the tunnel being very long.

So you dismiss any thought of exploring it further. To be honest, you're quite glad of the excuse! As you start walking again, waiting for the level-crossing to appear once more through the mist ahead, you suddenly hear what sounds like someone chuckling behind you. 'Do you think it's the ghost of one of those hijackers?' Miss Crumble asks tensely. 'Perhaps we're searching in completely the wrong area and he's mocking us!' You're sure there's a quite rational explanation for the sound, though, and you bravely turn your head . . . *Go to 136.*

41

Since you chose not to borrow the codebook from Mr Sporran's museum, you can only hope that the message *wasn't* written by one of the hijackers. For there's certainly no other way you can possibly work it out. As you all continue walking again, trudging through the thick bracken and heather, you become vaguely conscious of something following you. And it's soon much more than vaguely – you're certain of it! 'It can't be a ghost, surely?' you ask with a gulp as the bracken crackles a short distance behind you. You add nervously, 'Ghosts wouldn't make any sound as they walk, would they?' But your two so-called experts on ghosts have no answer for you. They're much too frightened! There's only one thing for it. You're going to have to turn your head and find out for yourself . . . *Go to 210.*

42

You're all just about to read the inscription on the monument when you think you see it shudder slightly! Spooks immediately runs a safe distance away, but the rest of you decide it must be your imagination. A heavy stone cross like this wouldn't move, surely? So you return your attentions to the inscription and Miss Crumble reads it out loud. She uses her dramatic, eerie 'seance' voice! 'The tragedy happened on the stormy night of—' she begins, almost in a chant, but then she suddenly stops. The monument appears to be shuddering again! You all run off towards Spooks. Is this a small earth tremor – or is someone or something making the cross vibrate? Very slowly, you turn your heads to find out . . . *Go to 286.*

43

Miss Crumble was right. The message obviously was written by one of the hijackers. For it works out as: *ALL THREE CRATES OF GOLD ARE HIDDEN IN SOME SORT OF BUILDING.* 'Ah, now we're getting somewhere!' the Professor exclaims, his eyebrows lifting excitedly above his spectacles. 'That should really narrow down our search from now on!' You are a little more wary about the message, however. You have no doubt that it was chiselled by one of the hijackers, but what you do doubt is whether it's true. Your experience of them so far is that they are far from honest! So you suggest to the others that you treat the message with a certain caution. *Go to 107.*

44

'That's strange,' Miss Crumble remarks with a frown as she studies her special dice. 'It doesn't seem to want us to follow *either* branch of the railway line. We're to bear off to the left instead!' The sky grows darker and darker as you all walk in this direction. The Professor suddenly remembers that he has a torch in his knapsack, though, and so your little group can just about see where it's going. After about half an hour or so, the torch's powerful beam suddenly picks out a tiny stone building ahead. It's a ruined church. 'Perhaps *that's* why the dice wanted us to come this way!' Miss Crumble remarks as you all hurry up to it. ***Go to 145.***

45

Miss Crumble studies her special dice, a deep frown developing on her plump face. 'I think it wants us to search the graveyard rather than the church,' she says, scratching her head. But when you all walk over to the door through which you came in, you find that it is securely locked! Is this the work of mischievous ghosts? It seems the only explanation. 'No need to panic,' the Professor says, trying to keep calm but as white in the face as the rest of you. 'All we have to do is use our key to unlock it again!'

Do you have either of the KEYS in the KNAPSACK CARD? If

you do, place it exactly over the door's 'lock' below – then follow the instruction. (You may try both KEYS if you have them.) If you don't have either of the KEYS – or your KEY doesn't work – go to 245 instead.

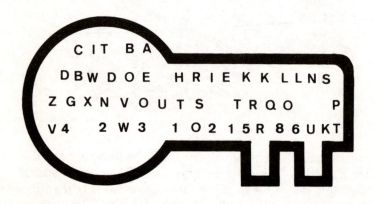

46

Your little group now quickly makes its way towards the two carriages, deciding you had better search them as well. 'We'll start with this one, shall we?' you suggest, peering in through the murky window at the shabby seats. But it looks so dark and eerie in there that you're all very nervous about opening the door. What if the carriage is full of ghosts? But *one* of you is going to have to lead the way into the carriage. Who are you going to choose? Miss Crumble, of course, suggests leaving it to her special dice . . .

Throw the SPECIAL DICE – then turn to the appropriate number.

If 💀 thrown   go to 222

If 🦇 thrown   go to 259

If 👻 thrown   go to 163

47

The Professor slowly descends the ladder, being careful not to lose his footing. Suddenly, though, he starts to come down a lot more quickly, almost not caring about his safety. He seems in a real panic! 'What on earth's wrong, Professor?' Miss Crumble asks as he nears the bottom of the signal. 'You look as if you've just seen a ghost!' The Professor puts a skinny hand to his heart, waiting until he has recovered some breath before speaking. 'That's exactly what I have done, Miss Crumble,' he replies in a quaking voice, 'just seen a ghost! It was when I looked up. Something was hovering just above the signal!' Not sure whether this was merely the Professor's imagination or not, you and Miss Crumble anxiously peer towards the top of the signal yourselves . . . ***Go to 302.***

48

When you have recovered from this haunting, record it on the GHOST COUNTER. Now go to 33.

49

You find yourself having to climb up the eerie-looking signal after all. For it's *you* that Miss Crumble's special dice chooses! You slowly mount the iron rungs, the wind seeming to become fiercer and fiercer as you near the top. Finally reaching the arm of the signal, you keep a nervous eye on it as you take in the view. But there *isn't* really any view. It's now so dark that you can see only a very short distance along the track. So you start making your way back to the bottom of the signal again, still expecting to hear that rusty arm suddenly shift position above you. If it does, you're sure the fright will make you fall right off the ladder! To your relief, though, the signal arm remains absolutely still. ***Go to 301.***

50

Quite how the little symbol showing on Miss Crumble's dice is meant to indicate a *direction*, you don't know! But she insists it *does* and so you just have to believe her. 'We're to head in that direction,' she says confidently, pointing her chubby finger to the right. 'A hundred metres or so,' she adds, 'and we should be right back at the railway line!' But your doubts about the ability of the special dice seem to be confirmed. You've walked a good two hundred metres now . . . and the railway line is still nowhere in sight. You do finally reach *something*, though – a huge Celtic cross. 'We can't be that far from the line,' the Professor remarks as he excitedly studies it. 'Look at this inscription down here. The cross is to commemorate the train disaster!'

Do you have the MAP in the KNAPSACK CARD? If you do,

use it to find which square the huge cross is in – then follow the instruction. If you don't, you'll have to guess which instruction to follow.

> If you think B2   go to 42
> If you think B1   go to 152
> If you think C1   go to 93

51

You all tensely start to examine the old locomotive. 'There's nothing to be scared of,' Miss Crumble remarks, trying to sound quite composed. 'This isn't the same train that was involved in the terrible accident, if that's what anyone is thinking. According to Mr Sporran, that train was never recovered. It's still at the bottom of the river.' Be that as it may, you can't help thinking it must have looked very similar to this one. And so the rusty locomotive still gives everyone the creeps! Walking round to the front, the Professor suddenly notices that something has been scratched into the paintwork, just above the buffers. It looks like a coded message!

Use the CODEBOOK CARD to find out what this message says by decoding the instruction below. If you don't have one, go to 78 instead.

52

Miss Crumble now tries the handle on the door again. This time it does turn and she eagerly squeezes into the washroom. Her plump body takes up so much space in there that you and the Professor decide you had better wait outside, leaving the search to her. There's not even enough room for Spooks to join his mistress! After a lot of clattering and knocking things over, Miss Crumble finally steps back out of the washroom. There's a broad grin on her face, making her double chin almost a triple one. 'Have you found the gold, Miss Crumble?' you ask excitedly. Unfortunately, she hasn't. But she *has* found something in the washroom – another copy of the hijackers' codebook!

If you don't already have it there, put the CODEBOOK into the KNAPSACK CARD. Now go to 134.

53

The lack of a key is no real obstacle, however. There are so many broken windows in the dilapidated building that it is quite easy for you to enter through one of them. You've all just crawled through the safest-looking of the broken windows when you hear a faint rumbling sound outside. It grows louder and louder. To begin with, you think it is just a distant roll of thunder but then Miss Crumble is convinced she can hear something else as well; a voice coming from the wind-swept platform! Is it the ghost of the old stationmaster warning passengers to keep to the back of the platform because a fast train is approaching? Hoping Miss Crumble's ears are deceiving her, you all tensely peer out of the broken window... ***Go to 226.***

54

When you have recovered from this haunting, record it on the GHOST COUNTER. Now go to 94.

55

'Perhaps there's another door at the back of the hut,' you suggest. So you all hurry round there, the dark sky exploding with thunder above you. You're in luck – there *is* another door. And you're even more lucky – this one's unlocked! You lead the way through the door, Miss Crumble and Spooks following closely behind. The Professor, however, stops outside for a moment, squinting into the distance. 'What is it, Professor?' you ask with concern. 'Have you seen something?' His bony face is as white as a sheet. 'Yes, I think I have,' he answers quietly. 'It was in that last flash of lightning. I'm sure I saw a train in that valley over there!' So you all anxiously wait for the valley to be lit up by the next flash . . . ***Go to 232.***

56

'Really! What's wrong with you, Professor Bones?' Miss Crumble exclaims reproachfully. 'That noise is just the wind whistling through the bridge's girders. Surely such a ghost expert as yourself should be able to tell whether it is a ghost train or isn't a ghost train?' The Professor is clearly relieved at this explanation of Miss Crumble's but quickly hides it. He pretends disappointment instead! 'Yes, you're right, Miss Crumble,' he apologises. 'I should be able to tell the difference between a ghost train and the wind. I suppose it was just wishful thinking on my part. Although I've seen lots of ghosts before, I've never actually seen a ghost *train*. Except at a funfair, of course!' **Go to 270.**

57

Your little group now leaves the church but, as you're passing through the overgrown graveyard, the Professor suddenly stops. 'That's strange,' he remarks, polishing his spectacles just to make sure he's seeing correctly. 'This tomb has a keyhole in it! You know what that suggests, don't you? It's not really a tomb at all but a secret hiding-place. Perhaps this is where the treasures of the church were hidden to save them from Highland bandits!' But you and Miss Crumble are wondering if there's something else now hidden in the false tomb – the hijackers' gold! You're only going to be able to find out, though, if you have the right key for it . . .

Do you have either of the KEYS in the KNAPSACK CARD? If

you do, place it exactly over the tomb's 'lock' below to see if it works – then follow the instruction. (You may try both KEYS if you have them.) If you don't have either of the KEYS – or your KEY doesn't work – go to 188 instead.

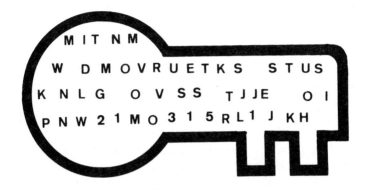

58

You're just explaining to the Professor that you didn't bring along Mr Sporran's map when you think you hear sniggering behind you. Could it be the ghost of one of the hijackers, mocking your attempt to find his gold? Or is it just the wind blowing through the thick bracken? Neither you nor Professor Bones are going to hang around to find out and you both hurry towards the cottage. You arrive there just as Miss Crumble is cautiously opening the door and you push her inside with you. 'What on earth is it, my dears?' she asks, startled, as you move over to one of the broken windows. You nervously peer into the mist outside, wondering if it *is* a ghost roaming about out there . . . ***Go to 124.***

59

The coded message works out as: *THERE ARE THREE CRATES OF GOLD HIDDEN. ALL ARE A SHORT DISTANCE BEFORE THIS BRIDGE.* Professor Bones looks like a delighted child as he returns the codebook to his knapsack. 'This proves that those rumours are true!' he exclaims in a high, excited voice, rubbing his hands together. 'One of the hijackers must have scratched this message down here just before reboarding the train. Of course, he wasn't going to have a very long journey. Another fifty metres or so and the train was in the water!' **Go to 177.**

60

Miss Crumble was right about there being an old, bearded face in the far corner of the hut. But it's in a picture frame. It was not a ghost she was looking at, but a portrait on the wall! The Professor walks over to the painting, shining his torch at the inscription underneath. It reads: *Robbie McTavish, 1761–1843*. 'Robbie McTavish must have been the man who started this mountain-rescue hut,' he says with fascination, tugging at his little beard. 'Look at that coil of climbing rope over his shoulder. And look at that craggy face. You only get a face like that from many years of battling the elements!' **Go to 109.**

61

Eagerly pushing the door open, you all step inside the small hut. 'I was right about it being a shelter for the workmen,' the Professor remarks on spotting an old stove in the corner. There's a battered kettle and two rusty tin mugs on it. 'What a shame I wasn't right about the gold as well,' he adds sadly, shaking his domed head. But then his eyebrows suddenly leap up above his spectacles as if he's just had another brainwave. 'Wait a minute!' he cries excitedly. 'Wait a minute! There are certainly no chests or crates in here – but perhaps the hijackers transferred the gold to the inside of that stove!' For a moment, you and Miss Crumble think the Professor might well be right, growing just as excited yourself. But all you're able to find in the old stove is another of the hijackers' codebooks!

If you don't already have it there, put the CODEBOOK CARD into the slit of the KNAPSACK CARD. Now go to 168.

62

Raising the lid of the box, you and Miss Crumble eagerly peer inside. 'Any gold there?' the Professor calls over, still more interested in the rusty levers at the other end of the signal box. You would bet anything that he owned a train set when he was young. In fact you would bet anything that he still did! 'No, I'm afraid there isn't, Professor,' you reply disappointedly. 'There are just lots of old paraffin lamps inside. Wait a minute, though. What's this folded sheet of paper down the side?' It's another map of the railway line!

If you don't already have it there, put the MAP into the KNAPSACK CARD. Now go to 321.

You all keep in a close huddle as you walk along the dark platform, sure that a ghost is suddenly going to leap out at you! The storm is at its fiercest yet, lightning repeatedly illuminating the eerie mountains all around. They seem to come closer and closer with every flash, but at last you reach the very end of the platform. You're all just wondering whether your scary excursion was worthwhile when Miss Crumble notices a large grit-box. Now this *would* have been a safe hiding-place for the few days the hijackers needed one. The box only would have been opened by the station staff when they needed to grit the ice in the depths of winter. So you all eagerly try to lift the lid of the large metal box. You can't understand why it won't open. But then you notice it is held down by a padlock!

Do you have either of the KEYS in the KNAPSACK CARD? If you do, place it exactly over the padlock's 'lock' below to see if it works – then follow the instruction. (You may try both KEYS if you have them.) If you don't have either of the KEYS – or your KEY doesn't work – go to 294 instead.

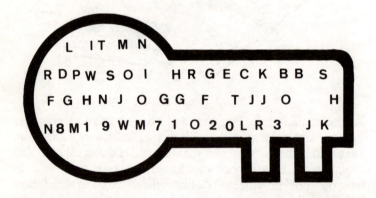

64

You now heave at the chest's lid again and it comes open. But that's as far as your joy goes because there are only mouldy dog biscuits inside! 'These must have been for the crofter's sheepdog,' Miss

Crumble remarks. 'I expect he locked them away because his dog kept sniffing them out and pinching them. I have the same problem with Spooks and my chocolate digestives!' But Spooks is taking no notice of his mistress, suddenly disappearing under the bed. Was he hoping to find some fresher dog biscuits down there perhaps? 'Now drop that dusty thing at once, Spooks!' Miss Crumble orders as he re-emerges with what looks like a thick crispbread in his mouth. It turns out to be something very different from a crispbread, though. It's a codebook!

If you don't already have it there, put the CODEBOOK into the KNAPSACK CARD. Now go to 312.

65

Your first haunting! When you have recovered from the shock, record it on the GHOST COUNTER. Now go to 127.

66

You all walk and walk, the loch a good hour behind you now, but there's *still* no sign of the railway line. This direction obviously wasn't such a good idea after all! 'Someone else should have chosen it,' the Professor grumbles wearily. 'It's all the fault of that dice of yours, Miss Crumble. I never did put any trust in it!' Miss Crumble is just about to come to the defence of her dice when you spot a large stone tower on the hill to your left. 'It looks like a folly of some sort,' you remark, glad to be able to interrupt this bickering. 'If we can find it on the map it will show us exactly where we are in relation to the railway line!'

Use the MAP to find which square the stone tower is in – then follow the appropriate instruction. If you don't have the MAP in the KNAPSACK CARD, you'll have to guess which instruction to follow.

<pre>
          If you think C3   go to 33
          If you think D3   go to 314
          If you think D4   go to 180
</pre>

67

'I'm sorry, my dear,' Miss Crumble informs you after she has rolled her special dice, 'but I'm afraid it has chosen *you*!' So, taking a deep nervous breath, you slowly start towards the bridge. You almost think you can hear the hijackers' screams as the train plunged off the end! But it's surely just a trick of the wind. 'Just in case they left a clue at the very last moment, I think we should actually venture on to the bridge,' you suggest as you reach it. 'But as soon as it starts to feel unsafe, we must make our way back again.' You gingerly tread from sleeper to sleeper, moving further and further out across the deep valley. Finally, you find the sort of thing you had been hoping for – a message scratched into the girders! But, unfortunately, it's in some sort of code . . .

Do you have the CODEBOOK in your KNAPSACK CARD? If you do, use it to find out what the message says by decoding the instruction below. If you don't, go to 195 instead.

68

The trap-door flaps down quite easily! Miss Crumble eagerly asks you and the Professor to help lift her up into the loft but you tactfully propose that it's *you* who should go up there. You're not sure that you'd be able to support Miss Crumble's weight! 'Any sign of a chest there?' the Professor excitedly calls up as you crawl through the loft, shining the torch in front of you. All you see to begin with is more rescue equipment – a few pairs of skis and a small sledge – but then you come across a mysterious heap under an old stretcher blanket. Pulling the blanket off, you reveal at least a dozen bars of gleaming gold. You've found it at last!

Well done! But don't forget that there is more than one stack of gold hidden near the railway line. If you would like to attempt to find the others as well you must start your exploration again from the beginning. Try setting off with a different ITEM next time.

69

There's suddenly an ominous creaking from directly underneath and you suggest leaving the bridge immediately. 'It sounds as if what's left of it might give way at any moment,' you remark, cautiously leading the way back to firm ground. Your little group now starts to follow the railway line in the other direction, away from the bridge. It seems to go on and on, endless in the thick mist. Eventually, though, a tall wooden hut looms out of the greyness ahead. It's a signal box, just to one side of the track. You all realise that this could be a good hiding-place for the gold, but the derelict hut is so eerie-looking that none of you really wants to lead you all towards it. Miss Crumble anxiously takes out her special dice, suggesting you all let *that* make the decision . . .

Throw the SPECIAL DICE – then turn to the appropriate number.

If ☠ thrown	go to 5
If 🦇 thrown	go to 175
If 👻 thrown	go to 115

When you have recovered from this haunting, record it on the GHOST COUNTER. Now go to 283.

71

All nervously turning and lifting your heads, however, you discover that it *isn't* a ghost responsible for that cry after all. It's just a large hawk gliding round above you. You're still not completely relaxed about it, though. 'Are you sure it won't suddenly turn *into* a ghost of some sort, Professor?' you ask him anxiously, staring up at the bird's huge flapping wings. But the Professor shakes his head knowledgeably. 'No, of course not, my dear child!' he tells you. 'There have been many cases of owls turning into ghosts, but never hawks as far as I can recall!' ***Go to 277.***

72

The coal-yard gates make a horrible creaking sound as you cautiously push them open. They obviously haven't been used for years. 'We need to search the biggest heaps of coal,' the Professor informs you both, rather pointing out the obvious, 'the ones that could hide a large chest.' You all tackle different heaps, kicking the individual lumps of coal aside. A good half-hour is spent on this mucky search – but there isn't so much as a *nugget* of gold in there. You're just leaving the coal-yard when you notice two white eyes staring at you all from the top of one of the heaps. They seem to have no face or body to them! 'They're ghost eyes!' Miss Crumble shrieks, again forgetting that she is meant to be quite used to ghosts. A little pink mouth then appears beneath the eyes, however, and a friendly bark comes out of it. It's just Spooks, covered in coal-dust! ***Go to 323.***

73

The tunnel becomes darker and darker. You'd hoped that you would be able to see the other end of the tunnel by now but it's obviously a lot longer than you'd thought. You're just about to suggest giving up and turning back when Miss Crumble suddenly falls flat on her face! 'Do stop fussing, Professor,' she tuts as he tries to help her up. 'You'd do better to have a look at what made me trip. Unless I'm much mistaken, it's a wooden chest!' Miss Crumble *isn't* mistaken – it is indeed a chest that tripped her up. And exactly the sort of chest that the railway would use for transporting gold. The only problem is that it's securely locked!

Do you have either of the KEYS in the KNAPSACK CARD? If you do, place it exactly over the chest's 'lock' below to see if it works – then follow the instruction. (You may try both KEYS if you have them.) If you don't have either of the KEYS – or your KEY doesn't work – go to 155 instead.

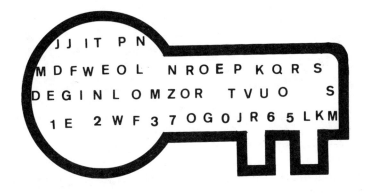

74

'You'd better keep hold of your torch, Professor,' Miss Crumble advises him after she has studied her special dice. 'I'm afraid it's you who must lead towards the station!' The Professor immediately starts to stride out in that direction just as another flash of lightning makes the spooky silhouette appear again! He reaches the derelict building and leads you all round to the station's main entrance. But when he tries to open the rotting door, he finds that it is locked! 'We're going to need a key,' he gulps as the sky eerily lights up once more . . .

Do you have either of the KEYS in the KNAPSACK CARD? If you do, place it exactly over the station door's 'lock' below to see if it works – then follow the instruction. (You may try both KEYS if you have them.) If you don't have a KEY – or your KEY doesn't work – go to 53 instead.

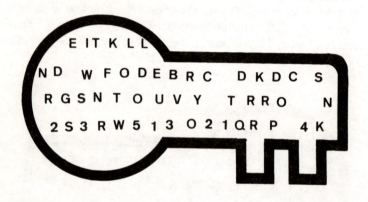

75

As you all anxiously peer up at the choir-stall, a large crow suddenly rises from it, disappearing through the open roof. It gives you quite a shock – but not half as much as a ghost would have done! 'So that's all it was!' the Professor exclaims with relief. 'It must have taken shelter up there because of this storm that seems to be brewing.' You all become rather concerned about the storm so you decide you had better move on from the church. Before you do, though, you return your attention to the collection box and turn it upside down to see if anything drops out through the coin slot. But it's quite empty! ***Go to 211.***

76

When you have recovered from this haunting, record it on the GHOST COUNTER. (Don't forget: when you have recorded four haunatings, you must immediately stop the adventure and start the game all over again.) Now go to 194.

77

Swinging open the unlocked door, you now climb inside the locomotive. The others join you in the driver's compartment; first Spooks, then Miss Crumble, then the Professor. You shine the Professor's torch round, hoping to spot the bars of gold in there somewhere. But you're to be disappointed. There are a couple of rusty shovels, a pile of oily rags, some loose coal on the floor . . . but that's all. You'll have to search elsewhere in the shed! *Go to 46.*

78

Unfortunately, of course, you didn't borrow the codebook from the museum – and so you can't tell whether this message was left by one of the hijackers. You hope it wasn't. Perhaps it was just scribbled there by an engineer working on the locomotive; perhaps a code he used to remind himself which parts to check. You soon have something else to think about, though. There's a loud screech from outside the engine shed. It sounds rather like a train suddenly having to do an emergency stop, just a few hundred metres up the line. Is this other locomotive the *ghost* one? You all step outside the shed again and anxiously peer along the line . . . **Go to 190.**

79

'Well, fancy that, it's chosen me!' Miss Crumble exclaims as she glances at her dice. 'To tell you the truth,' she confesses, 'I haven't a clue which is the best way back for the railway line. But my dice obviously knows best and so I'm going to suggest we head off to the right!' You're all just about to follow her away from the loch when you notice a dilapidated boathouse at the edge of the water. This would be the perfect hiding-place for the gold! So you all hurry towards the boathouse and start tugging the wooden door at the back. But you suddenly notice that it's padlocked.

Do you have either of the KEYS in the KNAPSACK CARD? If you do, place it exactly over the padlock's 'lock' below to see if it works – then follow the instruction. (You may try both KEYS if you have them.) If you don't have either of the KEYS – or your KEY doesn't work – go to 296 instead.

80

'I can't see any ghost,' you whisper nervously as you all peer towards the roof of the engine shed. But the horrible pounding noise continues, growing louder and louder. Then you suddenly realise what it is. 'It's just rain pounding on the *outside* of the roof,' you remark with relief. 'It's so noisy because the roof is made of metal. The storm must have started.' When you think about it, though, perhaps you shouldn't be too relieved at the explanation. A storm might be preferable to a ghost – but a storm is still cause for concern. Perhaps it will raise all the ghosts from that fateful night . . . perhaps you'll start seeing them everywhere now! ***Go to 134.***

81

'It says that we should take this branch that goes off to the right,' Miss Crumble informs you as she studies how her special dice fell. Again you wonder how she came up with such an interpretation. All you can see on the dice is a funny little skull and crossbones. Perhaps she chose this branch just because she thinks there is less chance of seeing the ghost train on it! Anyway, your little group now starts to follow this other line, wondering where it will lead. 'We did borrow

that map from the museum, didn't we?' Miss Crumble asks as you all trudge along. 'We ought to locate where the railway line divides.'

Use the MAP to find in which square the railway line divides – then follow the instruction. If you don't have the MAP in the KNAPSACK CARD, you'll have to guess which instruction to follow.

> If you think B2   go to 13
> If you think B3   go to 129
> If you think C3   go to 84

82

When you have recovered from this haunting, record it on the GHOST COUNTER. Now go to 51.

83

The Professor continues to lead you all through the mountain-rescue hut, nervously shining his torch round. Its beam falls on some stretchers and old climbing equipment, both covered in cobwebs. Then it picks out a rusty telescope positioned at the window. 'That would have been to keep an eye on the mountains,' the Professor informs you, 'so the people who manned this hut could check if anyone appeared to be stranded up there.' You and Miss Crumble are more interested in something else at the window, though. Lying on the ledge is a large green key!

If you don't already have it there, put the GREEN KEY into the KNAPSACK CARD. Now go to 109.

84

What's happening to Miss Crumble? you wonder. She's becoming as absent-minded as the Professor. Doesn't she remember you had all decided *not* to borrow the map from the museum? 'Oh yes, so we did,' she says when you remind her. 'My mind's on other things. I just saw a flash of light in the distance and I thought it might be the ghost train!' The Professor has a more rational explanation for the flash, though. 'I think you'll find it was just lightning, Miss Crumble,' he tells her. 'If you wait a moment,' he adds, 'you'll hear the thunder follow.' But as you all listen for the thunder, you hear a shrill whistle instead. Was Miss Crumble right about the ghost train after all? There's suddenly another flash in the distance . . . **Go to 262.**

85

'Now come along, Professor Bones,' Miss Crumble urges him, trying to get him moving again. 'There's absolutely no doubt about it, as far as I can see. That bridge we can see up there through the mist is the very one we're looking for. The exact same one where that terrible accident occurred!' So the Professor reluctantly heads towards the bridge once more, you and Miss Crumble following closely behind. Checking that Spooks is with you as well, you notice that he is carrying a very old notebook in his mouth. He must have found it on the ground. 'Look, it's just like the one that Mr Sporran showed us in the museum,' you remark as you take the notebook from the little dog. 'It's got lots of weird symbols and instructions. It's obviously another of the gang's codebooks!' There's only one thing that slightly concerns you, though. After all these years lying in the open, how is it that the book is still in such good condition?

If you don't already have it there, put the CODEBOOK CARD into the slit of the KNAPSACK CARD. Now go to 270.

86

'Don't worry – no ghost!' you announce with relief. 'That part of the bridge must have been about to collapse anyway and our weight just tipped the balance.' The Professor and Miss Crumble now both try to pretend that they hadn't been scared out of their wits after all. 'I knew there wouldn't be a ghost behind it,' the Professor says casually. 'That would have been hoping for far too much right at the beginning of our mission!' Miss Crumble is equally outrageous. 'Well, I felt the same, Professor,' she unashamedly lies. 'A big disappointment, of course, but there it is!' ***Go to 12.***

When you have recovered from this haunting, record it on the GHOST COUNTER. Now go to 19.

88

Having thrown open the lid of the iron chest, you all eagerly look inside. But it's only full of old train tickets! 'We should have known it wouldn't be the gold,' you remark disappointedly. 'It was hardly likely to have been left in a place as open as this.' As you now climb back to the top of the steep bank, the Professor has a think about those old tickets. 'I expect they were waiting in that chest to be shovelled into the steam-engine's boiler along with the coal,' he guesses, giving his little beard a tug. 'But the hijackers probably just chucked the chest overboard instead,' he adds. 'No respect for the countryside – that was their problem!' Miss Crumble quickly puts a finger to her lips and tells the Professor that he shouldn't speak any ill of the hijackers – not even calling them litter-louts. 'Their spirits are probably still floating around here,' she whispers gravely, 'and they're not likely to take kindly to being criticised!' ***Go to 193.***

89

'So *that's* what shut one of the gates!' the Professor chuckles with relief. 'It's just a shaggy Highland cow crossing the line. It obviously wandered a bit too close to that first gate. I don't think we'll be seeing the ghost train appear just yet after all!' The Professor suddenly remembers that a true ghostologist should be disappointed by this, however. 'Well, never mind,' he adds quickly. 'I'm sure we'll catch a glimpse of the ghost train eventually. We mustn't give up hope!' But it seems that even Spooks isn't taken in by this – let alone Miss Crumble and yourself – for the little dog gives a quiet yawn! **Go to 34.**

90

Your little group has walked about half a mile from the church when you arrive at a strange-looking stone wall. It's in the shape of an E. You all wonder what it was for but then the Professor suddenly clicks his bony fingers. 'I know!' he exclaims. 'It's quite obvious really, given that there were once several farms in this area. It's a shelter for cows or sheep, to protect them from these fierce winds. I wonder if it's shown on Mr Sporran's map?'

Use the MAP to find which square the animal shelter is in – then follow the instruction. If you don't have one, you'll have to guess which instruction to follow.

If you think C4	go to 18
If you think D4	go to 215
If you think D3	go to 140.

91

The coded message works out as: *GOLD NOT HIDDEN HERE BUT I'VE LEFT SOMETHING IN THE GUTTERING ABOVE THE FRONT DOOR. THIS WILL BE USEFUL IN THE SEARCH FOR THE GOLD.* You're not as delighted by this as might have been expected. For it means that you've got to return to the spooky cottage. You only hope that this 'something' is worth it! A few minutes later, you're cautiously running your fingers along the gutter, hoping that there aren't any rats up there. The only thing your fingers touch, though, is a rusty key. It's a large green one!

If you don't already have it there, put the GREEN KEY into the KNAPSACK CARD. Now go to 312.

92

When you have recovered from this haunting, record it on the GHOST COUNTER. Now go to 39.

93

The Professor starts to read out the inscription on the monument, his nose almost right up to it because of his short-sightedness. 'This is to commemorate the terrible rail tragedy that occurred in this misty glen,' he reads in his eager shrill voice. 'It happened on a stormy October night, the nearby bridge unable to stand up to the cruel elements. Eight men in all went down – eight villains who met their doom. May God rest their souls.' The Professor straightens up again, scratching his domed head in thought. 'Let me see now,' he considers quite merrily. 'October? That's the month we're in now, isn't it?' You, Miss Crumble and Spooks all stare at the Professor with annoyance. Yes, it *is* October now. And you really didn't want him to remind you about it, thank you very much! ***Go to 15.***

94

Your little group has walked only a few hundred metres further from the water tank when you spot a small building at the side of the railway line. It must be a station! But your delight wanes as the station comes nearer and nearer. There's an eerie silence about the dilapidated building, a silence broken only by the hissing of the wind through its broken windows. Then it looks even more forbidding as the storm suddenly starts. It becomes a haunting silhouette in the flashes of bright blue light . . . ***Go to 116.***

95

Tentatively starting to explore the vast interior of the engine shed, you notice two old carriages and a rusty locomotive. This must be very like the one that plunged off the bridge all those years ago. Perhaps it *is* the same one, in fact. Although it's still meant to be lying at the bottom of the river, perhaps it has eerily made its way back to this shed! In other words, this is not a real locomotive you're peering at . . . but a *ghost* one! You're scaring yourself unnecessarily, though, because Spooks bravely jumps up into the locomotive. It's as real as he is! As you all join him in the driver's compartment, the Professor points to where the coal was shovelled into the boiler. Strangely, there's a padlock on the little iron door there. Is this because the gold has been hidden inside?

Do you have either of the KEYS in the KNAPSACK CARD? If you do, place it exactly over the boiler door's 'lock' below to see if it works – then follow the instruction. (You may try both KEYS if you have them.) If you don't have either of the KEYS – or your KEY doesn't work – go to 218 instead.

96

Why did you have to suggest that Miss Crumble use her special dice? For it decides that *you* should be the one to take the lead into the engine shed! You walk nervously towards the narrow door at the side of the long building and slowly turn the handle. You are rather hoping that it will be locked... but it creaks open! As you step into the shed's vast dark interior, you anxiously turn round to make sure the others are still right behind you. Miss Crumble and Spooks are, but the Professor has stopped outside. 'I won't be a minute,' he calls. 'I'm just searching through my knapsack for the map. I thought I'd locate this engine shed so we know exactly where we are!'

Do you have the MAP in the KNAPSACK CARD? If you do, use it to find which square the engine shed is in – then follow the instruction. If you don't, you'll have to guess which instruction to follow.

If you think B3	go to 268
If you think A3	go to 159
If you think A2	go to 205

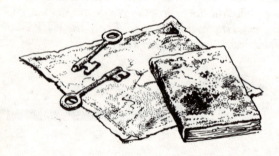

97

'I knew we were right to borrow this key from Mr Sporran!' you exclaim as you push open the little door. But the horrible creaking sound it makes half changes your mind. Perhaps it would have been better if you *weren't* able to enter the ruin after all! Nevertheless, you search every metre of the castle, up the spooky tower and down into the spooky dungeon. Alas, there's not a bar of gold in sight! 'I still say this would have been the perfect hiding-place for the hijackers,' the Professor remarks as you now leave the castle. 'The only reason it might not have been perfect,' he adds gloomily, 'is that it was just too far from the railway line. What I'm trying to say is that we're still well and truly out of our way!' **Go to 39.**

98

Fortunately, the next flash of lightning illuminates a small cottage a few hundred metres over to your right. You all hurry up to the door, noticing some faded writing there. It reads: *Mountain-Rescue Hut*. The hut obviously hasn't been used for ages, though, and so you're all rather nervous about entering. 'Well, someone's got to lead us in,' Miss Crumble remarks, just as there's another flash of lightning which splits a nearby tree in half. 'I think I'd better use my special dice!' she adds.

Throw the SPECIAL DICE – then turn to the appropriate number.

If ☠ thrown	go to 306
If 🦇 thrown	go to 217
If 👤 thrown	go to 169

99

You all impatiently open the door of the safe, hoping there's going to be a yellow glimmer inside – the glimmer of gold! But the safe just contains what the inscription on the outside says it contains –

lamps. 'We shouldn't be too disappointed,' the Professor says, suddenly having one of his brilliant ideas. 'If we can get one of these lamps to work it will mean that we can explore even deeper into the tunnel!' But that's the last thing you wanted . . . so perhaps it's not such a brilliant idea after all! 'No, I think we've explored the tunnel enough, Professor,' you tell him, starting to lead the way back again. 'It will be getting dark outside soon and there's probably a lot more of the railway line still to search.' **Go to 283.**

100

You haven't walked much further round the head of the loch when Spooks scampers off towards the reeds at the water's edge. He's spotted an old rowing-boat half-hidden amongst them. It's *extremely* old, in fact; so rotten that it looks as if it's about to fall apart. 'I wonder . . .' the Professor says, twiddling his moustache, deep in thought, as you all examine the boat. 'I wonder if the hijackers used this boat. Perhaps they hid one of the chests at the bottom of the loch!' There might well be something in the Professor's remark, for you suddenly notice what could be a coded message carved into the side of the boat.

Use the CODEBOOK CARD to find out what this message says

by decoding the instruction below. If you don't have the CODEBOOK in the KNAPSACK CARD, go to 132 instead.

101

'Well, spill the beans, Professor,' Miss Crumble urges impatiently when Professor Bones has used the codebook to try and make sense of the message. All her beads rattle with her excitement. 'Was it scribbled by one of the hijackers or not?' she demands. The Professor gives a thoughtful nod of his domed head. 'Oh yes,' he replies. 'It most certainly was. And I'm afraid there's been a bit of treachery from one of the hijackers here. The message says that one of the crates is *not* in the hiding-place he told the others. He was obviously intending to double-cross them!' ***Go to 243.***

102

'What a shame we didn't borrow Mr Sporran's codebook,' Miss Crumble sighs as you all disappointedly stare down at the symbols chiselled into the sleeper. 'I would bet my crystal ball that this was written by one of those dreadful hijackers!' You haven't left the sleeper far behind when you hear a scraping of metal coming from that direction. 'I told you those symbols were chiselled by one of the hijackers!' Miss Crumble exclaims, anxiously picking up Spooks and hugging him to her chest. 'His ghost is obviously sharpening his knife on the line.' But you tell Miss Crumble that the sound is probably just the creak of those level-crossing gates again. And to prove it, you insist that you all look round . . . ***Go to 172.***

103

Your little group continues to follow the eerie railway line, soon arriving at a large water tank. There's a long thick hose coming out of it and the Professor eagerly starts to examine this. 'The hose was for supplying the water to the trains,' he remarks, showing you how it could be swung from left to right to make the task easier. 'Steam-engines required quite a lot of water,' he adds. 'The water was needed to . . .' But his explanation stops as his rambling mind switches to something else. 'I've just had an idea!' he exclaims. 'If we can find this water tank on the map, it will show us exactly where we are!'

Use the MAP to find which square the water tank is in – then follow the instruction. If you don't have the MAP in the

KNAPSACK CARD, you'll have to guess which instruction to follow.

If you think A3   go to 221
If you think B3   go to 14
If you think B4   go to 287

104

Having used the key you and the Professor brought to her, Miss Crumble now eagerly moves her hands to the lid of the chest. It's absolutely freezing in the river but you're so excited you hardly notice. All your attention is on that iron box at the bottom of the water. As Miss Crumble's plump fingers now flip open the lid, you expect to see a golden glow shimmer up at you from the river-bed. But the chest only contains wooden floats. 'The chest must have once belonged to a fisherman,' the Professor remarks as you all make your way back, shivering, to little Spooks who is waiting on the bank. Miss Crumble's dog is obviously the only one of you with any sense! ***Go to 17.***

105

You're about to tell the Professor that you agreed not to take Mr Sporran's map. But Miss Crumble stops you by putting a chubby finger to her lips. She wants the Professor to find this out for himself, presumably as some sort of lesson for his continual forgetfulness! He searches right through his knapsack, from top to bottom, and then starts to search again. 'Now where did I put it?' he says, still not realising that he hadn't put it anywhere! Just as that fact finally dawns on him, you and Miss Crumble suddenly spot something coming towards you from the darkness of the tunnel. It's something white and shapeless! **Go to 244.**

106

When you have recovered from this haunting, record it on the GHOST COUNTER. Now go to 46.

107

You haven't followed the railway line much further when it suddenly divides. One track continues straight ahead while the other branches sharply off to the right. 'Which should we follow?' you ask, looking anxiously up at the sky. Although the mist has lifted quite a bit it's now beginning to get dark. And it also looks as if a storm is about to break – exactly as it did on the night of that disaster all those years ago. You haven't witnessed the ghost train yet, of course, but if there is such a thing you somehow feel that it's going to appear very soon now! Miss Crumble obviously thinks the same because her hand trembles as she takes out her special dice. 'We'll let this decide which branch we should follow,' she says nervously.

Throw the SPECIAL DICE – then turn to the appropriate number.

If ☠ thrown   go to 81

If 🦇 thrown   go to 299

If 👻 thrown   go to 44

108

You and Miss Crumble are still eagerly waiting for the Professor to decode the message on the lever. You're sure it would be much quicker if one of you two consulted the codebook but the Professor insists that it be him. 'Deciphering coded messages is a very complicated business,' he says as he slowly turns through the codebook's pages, scratching his head and tugging at his beard. 'It really needs a very scientific mind like mine. Ah! I think I've cracked it at last. Mmm . . . or have I? Yes, this is it. The message says that we should follow the main part of the railway line for the gold.' But that, of course, was exactly what you had been doing anyway. So the Professor's efforts were all a waste of time! **Go to 194.**

109

You've now thoroughly searched the inside of the hut. You'd really hoped that one of the chests of gold would be in there, but there's not a chest or box to be found. As you're all waiting for the storm to subside a little, though, Spooks starts to bark, looking up at the ceiling. 'Good gracious!' the Professor exclaims, as you all glance up there yourselves and notice a trap-door. 'There's a loft to the hut. We didn't consider that, did we?' No, you certainly didn't and you all hurriedly move an old table under the trap-door so you can reach it. 'Blow!' Miss Crumble exclaims as she tugs the little handle on the door. 'It's firmly locked. It obviously needs a key!'

Do you have either of the KEYS in the KNAPSACK CARD? If you do, place it exactly over the trap-door's 'lock' below to see if it works – then follow the instruction. (You may try both KEYS if you have them.) If you don't have either of the KEYS – or your KEY doesn't work – go to 216 instead.

110

'It suggests we search at the back of the church,' Miss Crumble remarks as she studies her special dice. 'Perhaps we'll find a secret chamber in the wall,' she adds excitedly, 'just like we did in that chapel at Ghostly Towers. And perhaps one of the chests of gold will be hidden inside!' So you all tap the back wall of the church but it sounds perfectly solid. It's then that the Professor notices a slim wooden box, standing about a metre high. There's a deep slot in the top. 'I know what it is!' he exclaims after scratching his domed head for a while. 'It's a collection box. You drop your coins through the slot and they would collect down here. The vicar would take them out by opening this little door.' When the Professor tries to open the door himself, however, he finds that it is locked!

Do you have either of the KEYS in the KNAPSACK CARD? If you do, place it exactly over the collection box's 'lock' below to see if it works – then follow the instruction. (You may try both KEYS if you have them.) If you don't have either of the KEYS – or your KEY doesn't work – go to 213 instead.

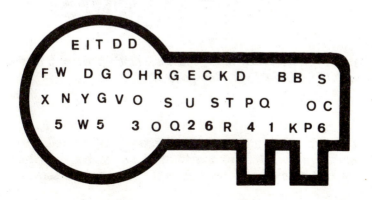

111

You all nervously raise the lid of the tomb. What if it's not a fake at all but a real one and there's a dry old skeleton inside! To everyone's relief there *isn't* a skeleton in there – but there isn't anything else either. Certainly no gold! So you all leave the graveyard, glad to see the back of that eerie place. You haven't walked far, however, when Miss Crumble suddenly lets out a scream. 'Spooks,' she cries, 'he's not here! He must have jumped into that tomb without us noticing and is trapped inside!' But in actual fact Spooks is trotting along happily just to one side of Miss Crumble. She has become such a bundle of nerves that she just didn't notice! **Go to 18.**

112

When you have recovered from this haunting, record it on the GHOST COUNTER. Now go to 57.

113

You were all expecting to see a ghost in sooty overalls shovelling coal into the boiler. But, fortunately, there *isn't* a ghost boilerman standing on the locomotive. So what *had* caused the shovel to clatter? It was Spooks! You suddenly spot his guilty face staring out at you from the locomotive. He must have stayed behind in the driver's compartment and accidentally knocked over one of the shovels. You wonder if Miss Crumble is going to give him a good telling-off for scaring you all like that. But she's so relieved that it's not a ghost that she just gives him a huge hug instead. You wonder if the poor dog might have preferred a telling-off, though, because he looks completely winded by the massive embrace! ***Go to 46.***

114

While the Professor is decoding the message on the water tank, you suddenly have a thought. The tank would be a wonderful hiding-place for the gold! So you quickly climb up the side and lean over the top. It's full of blackish water, but that still doesn't mean the gold isn't in there. Perhaps the bars have been dropped to the bottom. You're just about to suggest that you open the hose to empty the tank when the Professor announces that he has finally worked out the coded message. 'It says that the gold is at least half a mile away,' he informs you. Well, so much for your good idea! ***Go to 94.***

115

A sympathetic Miss Crumble informs you that her special dice has chosen *you* to lead the way to the signal box. So you take a deep breath and start to walk with as much courage as possible. This courage quickly drains away, however, as you reach the spooky building and climb the creaking wooden steps up its side. Your hand shakes as you put it to the narrow wooden door at the top. Perhaps the signalman's ghost will be there, still moving the levers up and down. Much to your relief, you find that the door is firmly locked. But then you think of the gold again. You really are going to have to try and open that door . . .

Do you have either of the KEYS in the KNAPSACK CARD? If you do, place it exactly over the door's 'lock' below to see if it works – then follow the instruction. If you don't have either of the KEYS – or your KEY doesn't work – go to 288 instead.

116

The storm grows fiercer and fiercer and you decide that you have no option but to take cover in the eerie station. But who is going to *lead* the way towards it? The Professor suddenly remembers that he'd packed a torch in his knapsack and he offers that to anyone who is prepared to go first. There are still no volunteers, though. 'There's only one thing for it, then,' Miss Crumble announces gravely as she reaches into her pocket. 'I'll have to let my special dice choose someone!'

Throw the SPECIAL DICE – then turn to the appropriate number.

If ☠ thrown	go to 74
If 🦇 thrown	go to 146
If 👻 thrown	go to 253

117

'Well, at least I was right about this being an emergency toolbox,' the Professor says with a disappointed shake of his bony head. 'Look, there are all sorts of tools inside: crowbars, pickaxes, sledge hammers. It's just such a shame there isn't any gold in here as well!' He pushes the metal door shut, locking it again before returning the key to his knapsack. 'Now, I think we should make our way back to the entrance,' he recommends. 'It's becoming difficult to see. If only I had thought to bring a torch with me. Then we could have gone much further down the tunnel.' But you happen to know that the Professor *does* have a torch with him. You spotted it in his knapsack! Was this his absent-mindedness again, or was he deliberately deceiving you and Miss Crumble? You decide to keep quiet about the matter, however. The fact is you're just as keen to leave this spooky tunnel yourself! ***Go to 267.***

118

The last to peep out from between his fingers is the Professor. 'Don't worry, Professor,' you tell him with a huge sigh of relief. 'There *isn't* any ghost train in front of us. It was obviously just a flash of lightning that made the shed vibrate. There must have been a direct strike on the roof.' The Professor coyly drops his hands from his face and straightens his tie. 'I must say, I thought it probably was,' he remarks. 'That's why I was so nervous. I've always had this deep fear of lightning, you see. Quite surprising, isn't it, from someone who wouldn't turn so much as a hair at encountering a ghost?' **Go to 134.**

119

'Now come on, Professor!' Miss Crumble chides him. 'You know full well that we didn't bring Mr Sporran's map with us. The special dice can't be tricked, you know. If it decides you must lead, Professor, then I'm afraid you *must*!' So the Professor coyly continues walking towards the signal box but he's only advanced a few more metres when Spooks gives a worried growl. There's a faint whining sound behind you. 'It's as if someone is playing bagpipes,' Miss Crumble observes nervously, 'but someone without much breath!' Of course, you all know what sort of person doesn't have much breath – a ghost! Hoping you're wrong, you slowly turn your heads to find out the cause of the whine . . . **Go to 38.**

120

'Well, I'm sure there's nothing very interesting inside,' Miss Crumble tries to reassure everyone when you realise that there's no way of opening the chest. 'It probably just contains the crofter's boots and shoes. I expect they were the most valuable possessions the poor man had!' You are just pushing the chest back under the bed (although you don't really know why since it's obvious that the crofter has long since deserted his cottage) when you hear a spine-chilling sound from outside. It's the loud, eerie baying of a dog! 'It must be the ghost of the crofter's old sheepdog,' the Professor remarks through chattering teeth. 'Perhaps he doesn't like us disturbing his master's home.' You all creep back to the front door and open it slightly. At any moment, you expect to see huge white fangs appearing out of the mist . . . ***Go to 36.***

121

This time Miss Crumble's dice chooses the Professor. You, Miss Crumble and Spooks watch his thin figure stroll off rather reluctantly towards the cottage. He almost disappears in the mist. 'Why is he hesitating at the door?' Miss Crumble asks bossily as you peer after him. 'I hope he's not having second thoughts about going inside. My special dice doesn't like it when someone doesn't do what it says. It will only pick Professor Bones again and again, every single time.' She wanders off after the Professor to warn him about this and you and Spooks decide you might as well follow. When you all arrive at the cottage, however, you find the reason for the Professor's delay. There are some symbols which could be a coded message carved into the door and he's trying to work them out!

*Use the **CODEBOOK** to find out what this message says by decoding the instruction below. If you don't have the **CODEBOOK CARD** in the **KNAPSACK CARD**, go to 260 instead.*

122

'Oh, my poor poppet!' Miss Crumble exclaims as you see not a ghost tapping furiously at the cottage window but *Spooks*. 'We'd forgotten all about him. We obviously trapped him inside when we closed the door behind us.' She immediately rushes back into the cottage, sweeping up the indignant Spooks into her arms again. 'Here's my little darling,' she announces as she joins you and the Professor outside once more. She starts to smother the poor little dog with kisses. 'Whatever was naughty mummy thinking of leaving you inside?' she scolds herself. But much more of that smothering and it looks as if Spooks will be desperately scampering back there! ***Go to 312.***

123

'Spooks!' you all exclaim letting out a sigh of relief together as his little white face suddenly appears in the signal box. So it was *him* padding up the steps. You were all so preoccupied with the oak box that none of you realised he was missing. And now you know *why* he went missing. For there's a thick iron bar between his teeth. Miss Crumble's clever little dog had obviously gone searching outside for something that could force open the box. Unfortunately, though, his initiative was all for nothing. When you use the iron bar to lever up the lid of the box, you find that there are only empty oil cans inside. **Go to 321.**

124

When you have recovered from this haunting, record it on the GHOST COUNTER. Now go to 9.

125

'We don't need the map to work out what the hut was for,' Miss Crumble calls back to you both, having impatiently waddled up to the tiny building to peer through its dilapidated door. 'There are lots of old tools inside. It was obviously used by the workmen who did repair jobs on the railway line. I wonder if any of their ghosts are about?' You and the Professor are quite sure that there *aren't*, though, and you therefore hurry along to join Miss Crumble at the hut. If there were any ghosts, she would surely have run a mile from the place. You'd learnt from your trip to Ghostly Towers that Miss Crumble was always a lot happier talking about ghosts than actually meeting them! ***Go to 168.***

126

Miss Crumble's special dice is clearly also of the view that, since it was the Professor's idea, he should be the one to climb the signal. For *he* is the one it picks! As he slowly starts to ascend the rusty ladder, he looks rather annoyed with himself. He's obviously wishing that he'd kept his mouth shut. 'I'm afraid it's too dark to see very far,' his frail, nervous voice finally calls down when he reaches the top. 'Perhaps this signal would be more useful to us if we looked for it on the map!'

Use the MAP to find which square the signal is in – then follow the instruction. If you don't have the MAP in the KNAPSACK CARD, you'll have to guess which instruction to follow.

If you think A2   go to 103
If you think B2   go to 47
If you think B3   go to 273

127

After following the eerie railway line for some half-mile or so, you all arrive at a small shed. It is just to one side of the line and looks as if it's been constructed from old sleepers. 'This must be where the track workmen took cover from any bad weather,' the Professor remarks as you all search round inside. 'Look at that old stove in the corner and those rusty tea mugs!' But you, Miss Crumble and Spooks are much more interested in a large iron box in the other corner. Could this be where some of the gold is hidden? When you try to lift the lid of the box, however, you discover that it is locked. Will one of those two keys will open it?

Do you have either of the KEYS in the KNAPSACK CARD? If you do, place it exactly over the box's 'lock' below to see if it works – then follow the instruction. If you don't have either of the KEYS – or your KEY doesn't work – go to 32 instead.

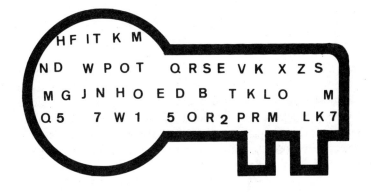

128

You now follow Miss Crumble into the spooky tunnel. There's an eerie dripping sound coming from somewhere and every one of your footsteps makes a horrible echo. Miss Crumble's are the worst because of the stout 'sensible' shoes she's wearing (you've already had a good lecture from her on the unsuitability of your trainers!). Suddenly, the Professor slips on the damp ground. Far from being sympathetic, Miss Crumble starts to give *him* a lecture on proper footwear as well. But he interrupts her, holding up a large green key. 'If I hadn't had poor shoes, Miss Crumble,' he lectures back defiantly, 'I wouldn't have fallen over. And if I hadn't fallen over, I wouldn't have found this on the ground!'

If you don't already have it there, put the GREEN KEY into the KNAPSACK CARD. Now go to 73.

129

You only have to walk a short distance further before you realise the purpose of this branch line, for it leads into a long shed. This was obviously where trains not in use were repaired and sheltered. You're going to have to explore the shed, of course – it would be a wonderful hiding-place for the gold. On the other hand, though, it's a very scary-looking building; its rusty corrugated iron rattling in the wind. You're all very reluctant to take the lead. Even when the Professor suddenly remembers that he'd packed a torch in his knapsack, there are *still* no volunteers. So you ask Miss Crumble to let her special dice pick someone.

Throw the special dice – then turn to the appropriate number.

        If 💀 thrown   go to 151

        If 🦇 thrown   go to 319

        If 👻 thrown   go to 96

130

Your first haunting! When you have recovered from the shock, record it on the GHOST COUNTER. Now go to 177.

131

The coded message at the side of the tunnel works out as: *YOU'RE LOOKING IN THE WRONG PLACE, MATES. THE GOLD IS HIDDEN MUCH NEARER THE RAILWAY LINE!* The Professor shakes his domed head sadly. 'So this detour has all been for nothing,' he says, tutting disappointedly. But you and Miss Crumble aren't as trusting as the Professor. 'This message was clearly left here by one of the hijackers,' you remark, 'but how do we know that he wasn't lying? It might have just been to put people on a false trail!' So you decide it best simply to ignore the message – it might be true, it might not – and continue on your exploration of the tunnel. ***Go to 27.***

132

Without a codebook, however, it's impossible to tell whether this message was left by the hijackers or not. 'Let's just hope it was carved by someone else and is perfectly innocent,' you remark as you all continue on your way. 'For instance, a fisherman who used the rowing-boat,' you add. 'Perhaps those strange symbols were just his unusual method of recording his catch.' But you are very soon wondering whether it *was* the hijackers after all. For you haven't left the rowing-boat far behind when there's a splashing sound coming from that direction. Is it the ghost of one of the hijackers working the oars? Or is it just a wild duck or goose flexing its wings? You very slowly turn your heads . . . ***Go to 178.***

133

'It looks as if I was right about this once being a railway tunnel,' the Professor remarks, pointing to a long, slender, metal box fastened to the damp wall. 'Look – this box has *Railway Property* written on it. It must have contained emergency tools for the line.' Wondering if it might now contain some of the gold instead, you all eagerly tug at the door of the box. But it's firmly locked.

Do you have either of the KEYS in the KNAPSACK CARD. If you do, place it exactly over the door's 'lock' below to see if it works – then follow the instruction. (You may try both KEYS if you have them.) If you don't have either of the KEYS – or your KEY doesn't work – go to 278 instead.

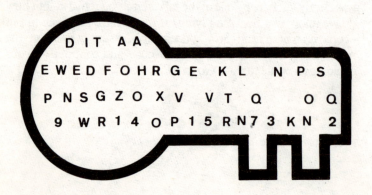

134

Something suddenly occurs to you. 'What idiots we are!' you exclaim, clapping a hand to your head. 'Why on earth are we investigating these carriages? *They* wouldn't have been a suitable hiding-place for the gold. Although this engine shed was obviously abandoned soon after the bridge disaster, the hijackers weren't to know that. They would have expected the carriages and locomotive still to be in service for a good while. So they were hardly going to hide their gold in them, were they? It would have been immediately found again!' The Professor and Miss Crumble agree that you have a very good point. But it's a point that leaves you all rather dispirited. Where do you start searching for the gold now? ***Go to 307.***

135

Making excited little sounds as she flicks through the hijackers' codebook, Miss Crumble finally deciphers the message as: *GOLD IS HIDDEN INSIDE THIS ENGINE SHED. BUT I AIN'T GOING TO TELL YOU WHERE EXACTLY. YOU'LL JUST HAVE TO HUNT FOR IT!* Greatly encouraged by this, she's now much more eager about entering the shed and quickly squeezes herself through the gap in the doorway. But when the rest of you have joined her inside the huge shed, her eagerness has already left her again. You immediately see why. The dark, silent interior has one of the eeriest atmospheres you've ever encountered! ***Go to 95.***

136

When you have recovered from this haunting, record it on the GHOST COUNTER. Now go to 283.

137

'Now, let's hope I can remember what the coded symbols looked like – and which order they were in,' Miss Crumble says when she has made her way back to the bottom of the signal. She excitedly takes the codebook from the Professor, flicking through its pages. 'Well, you were absolutely right, Professor!' she tells him a few minutes later as she returns the codebook. 'There *is* a station a little further along this line. The coded message says that it is exactly one mile away!' As you all continue along the track, you wonder if that means that the station has a special significance. In other words . . . could it be where the hijackers' gold is hidden? ***Go to 103.***

138

The ruined church is still only a short distance behind you when Miss Crumble thinks she hears voices coming from that direction.

'What sort of voices, Miss Crumble?' the Professor asks rather disbelievingly. But then the Professor hears them as well, and so do you. They sound like the quiet, respectful voices of people on their way to a service. 'But we know that there aren't any people round here,' you remark, desperately trying to think of some other explanation, 'and a service obviously hasn't been held in the church for centuries!' Yet what else can those voices be? You all anxiously turn your heads to find out . . . **Go to 304.**

139

'The special dice has told us to put our trust in Spooks and follow *him*,' Miss Crumble informs you as she picks it up again, returning it to her pocket. 'It says *he* will know the way to the railway line,' she continues. But when you glance down at Spooks, he certainly doesn't *look* as if he knows the way. In fact he appears as lost and puzzled as the rest of you! 'Are you sure you're doing the right thing making Spooks lead, Miss Crumble?' you ask hesitantly as you all start to follow the reluctant little dog. But Miss Crumble insists that her special dice always knows best. Spooks has trotted reluctantly along for some quarter of a mile when he nearly bumps into a large stone Celtic cross. 'Look at these symbols scribbled here. Do you think they could form some sort of coded message?' Professor Bones asks, excitedly examining the cross. 'Perhaps they were done by one of the hijackers!'

Use your CODEBOOK CARD to find out what the message says by decoding the instruction below. If you don't have the CODEBOOK CARD in the KNAPSACK CARD, go to 264 instead.

140

'What's that noise?' the Professor asks, suddenly peering into the darkness. 'It sounds like moaning.' But Miss Crumble starts to chuckle at his nervousness. '*Mooing* more like, Professor!' she mocks him. 'It's probably just one of those cows you were telling us about. With this storm about to break at any moment, I expect it wants to make use of the shelter.' But Miss Crumble has soon become as frightened as the Professor. For the next moan doesn't sound like a cow at all, and it appears to be coming from above. So, unless the cow is able to fly, it would seem that a ghost is about to appear! *Go to 187.*

141

Even vigorous kicks from you all won't open the locked washroom door. 'Perhaps we can get in from the outside of the carriage,' you suggest. 'We might be able to force down the window.' So you all follow Miss Crumble out of the carriage again. As you're hurrying round to the washroom window, however, the whole engine shed suddenly starts vibrating. What on earth's happening? Is the ghost train thundering towards the shed? You all cover your eyes, not daring to look. But then the vibration stops. Does that mean the ghost train is *inside* the shed now, standing right in front of you? One by one, you gradually peep between your fingers . . . ***Go to 118.***

142

When you have recovered from this haunting, record it on the GHOST COUNTER. Now go to 66.

143

Having pushed the door open, you warily lead the way into the hushed ticket office. Your torch beam falls on a couple of old chairs and a broken table. It then moves through the dusty darkness towards an ancient filing cabinet against the back wall. You all eagerly pull open the drawers of the cabinet, hoping that some of the gold has been transferred there, but they contain just crumbling rolls of tickets. As you're about to step out of the ticket office again, your torch beam lights up something else. It's a railway porter watching you from the corner! But your hearts all freeze for nothing. It isn't a real porter at all, or even a ghost one. It's just a porter's uniform – his musty jacket and cap – hanging from a coat-hook! **Go to 248.**

144

The scratched message decodes as: *RETURN TO START OF BRIDGE AND LOOK UNDER LARGE ROCK JUST TO LEFT OF RAILWAY LINE*. So you all hurriedly retrace your steps, wondering if you're going to find the gold already. 'It's my guess that the hijackers knew that the bridge was about to go when they scratched that message,' the Professor says excitedly as you now search for the rock. 'It was probably too late to flee the bridge by then,' he adds, 'and so they spent their last frantic seconds leaving a clue!' Unfortunately, though, it's not a clue to the whereabouts of the gold. For when you find the large rock and heave it over, there's just a rusty green key underneath!

If you don't already have it there, put the GREEN KEY into the KNAPSACK CARD. Now go to 12.

145

Having reached the ruined church, you all quickly walk round it, looking for an entrance. There seems a good chance that the gold will be hidden in there. 'Of course, it wouldn't be a very *proper* place to conceal stolen goods,' Miss Crumble remarks disapprovingly. 'A church should be sacred. But I don't suppose those dreadful hijackers would have given much thought to that.' You and the Professor are not really listening to her, however. You've arrived at a small oak door and you eagerly turn the handle. The door won't give, though. It's obviously locked.

Do you have either of the KEYS in the KNAPSACK CARD? If you do, place it exactly over the church door's 'lock' below to see if it works – then follow the instruction. (You may try both KEYS if you have them.) If you don't have either of the KEYS – or your KEY doesn't work – go to 269 instead.

146

Miss Crumble's face shows up stark white in the next flash of lightning. The special dice has obviously chosen her to lead towards the eerie station. 'Come on, Spooks!' she orders quietly as she waddles off in that direction. The little dog reluctantly trots up to her side, you and the Professor follow a short way behind them. Miss

Crumble soon arrives at the entrance to the station and tensely opens the little door there. But before she enters the hushed darkness, she suggests looking for the station on the map.

Use the MAP to find which square the station is in – then follow the instruction. If you don't have the MAP in the KNAPSACK CARD, you'll have to guess which instruction to follow.

        If you think A3   go to 230
        If you think A4   go to 189
        If you think B4   go to 316

147

The Professor has led you only a little nearer the derelict signal box when he finds another excuse for stopping. Or rather, Spooks does! For, sniffing between the sleepers, he discovers a large orange-coloured key amongst the weeds. 'Well done, Spooks!' the Professor praises him, giving him a little pat on the head. 'This key looks exactly the same shape as that orange one Mr Sporran showed us at the museum. So it could well be useful to us.' He gives Spooks another eager pat. 'Well done,' he repeats, 'I wish I had a dog like you.' But whether Spooks would wish for a master like the dotty Professor is quite another matter!

If you don't already have it there, put the ORANGE KEY into the KNAPSACK CARD. Now go to 241.

148

When you have recovered from this haunting, record it on the GHOST COUNTER. Now go to 39.

149

When the hooting starts again, however, you realise that it's coming from the crofter's cottage you just visited. Your eyes are drawn to the very top of the thatched roof . . . where there's a large owl blinking back at you! As Spooks frightens it away with his fiercest bark, you all chuckle with relief. 'So that's all it was, an owl!' the Professor exclaims. 'You know, I wonder if that's the simple explanation behind *all* these supposed ghost train experiences. People in a remote area like this often tend to be very gullible.' But did the Professor really believe that, you wonder, or was it just his wishful thinking? *Go to 312.*

150

Having pushed open the door, you cautiously lead the way into the signal box. It's spooky inside! There's a long row of rusty levers, covered in thick trailing cobwebs, and nearly every pane of glass in the wide observation window is broken. Your search doesn't produce any gold, unfortunately, but it's not completely in vain. 'Hey, look here!' you call to the others as you examine one of the mouldy walls. 'There's a large orange key hanging from a hook. Perhaps it would be a good idea to take it with us!'

If you don't already have it there, put the ORANGE KEY into the KNAPSACK CARD. Now go to 265.

151

'It's *me* the special dice has chosen, isn't it?' the Professor asks Miss Crumble gloomily, after she has studied how it rolled. She quietly nods her head at him. 'I knew it would be,' he says with a timid gulp, 'I just knew it would be!' Nevertheless, he immediately braces himself for the exploration of the eerie shed and leads you all towards it. There's a huge folding steel door at the front and he grabs hold of the handle at the far right of it in order to draw it open. You're sure there's a certain relief on his face as he announces that it is firmly locked!

Do you have either of the KEYS in the KNAPSACK CARD? If you do, place it exactly over the folding door's 'lock' below to see if it works – then follow the instruction. (You may try both KEYS if you have them.) If you don't have either of the KEYS – or your KEY doesn't work – go to 251 instead.

152

The stone cross *might* be to commemorate the railway disaster – but it certainly doesn't help you find the railway. 'I thought you said that it would mean we weren't far from the line, Professor,' Miss Crumble accuses him as you continue to search for it, walking away from the cross. The Professor can't resist answering back. 'And I thought *you* said, Miss Crumble,' he reminds her, 'that your special dice would help us find the line.' Their bickering suddenly stops, however. There's a strange wailing noise behind you – coming from the direction of that stone monument. Is it just that the wind has got fiercer? Or is there a ghost hovering round the cross . . .? ***Go to 286.***

153

Your little group hasn't walked much further from the needle of rock when you hear a slight tinkling sound just behind you. None of you dares turn round to find out what it is, but there are certainly some theories. 'Perhaps it's one of the hijackers' ghosts clinking the coins in his pocket,' Miss Crumble suggests nervously. The Professor is not to be outdone. 'Perhaps it's the ghost of the old porter, fiddling with his whistle chain,' he says with equal anxiety. In fact it's neither of these. Spooks suddenly notices his mistress's shoe, and the loop of string caught round it. On the end of the string is a rusty orange key which is tinkling along the rocky ground!

If you don't already have it there, put the ORANGE KEY into the KNAPSACK CARD. Now go to 277.

154

When you have recovered from this haunting, record it on the GHOST COUNTER. Now go to 90.

155

The Professor picks up the chest and carries it in his skinny arms. 'Since we don't have the means to unlock it,' he says, 'I suggest we take it back to the railway line with us. We might find an old iron bar or something along the track and we can try forcing it open.' It's only when your little group has left the tunnel and is well on its way back to the level-crossing that the Professor suddenly realises something. If the chest is that easy to carry, then there couldn't possibly be any gold inside. You and Miss Crumble were wondering how long it would take him to work this out! Rather huffily, the Professor drops the chest to the ground. But you haven't left it far behind when you think you hear chuckling coming from that direction. Is it the ghost of one of the hijackers having a good laugh at the Professor? You all nervously look over your shoulders to check . . . **Go to 310.**

156

The coded message works out as: *DIG STRAIGHT DOWN DIRECTLY BELOW THIS MESSAGE.* You all look at each other in anticipation. Is this where one of the chests of gold is buried? Perhaps you don't need to find your way back to the railway line after all! Miss Crumble immediately sets Spooks to work at scooping up the earth at the bottom of the signpost. The little dog digs as hard as he can, hoping that he will very soon be able to leave this horrible misty place. But it won't be just yet, unfortunately. For the only thing he finds down there is a large orange-coloured key!

If you don't already have it there, put the ORANGE KEY into the KNAPSACK CARD. Now go to 66.

157

'Oh, it's picked me!' Miss Crumble declares with a certain surprise after she has studied her special dice. She was obviously hoping that it would have insisted on the Professor. You're expecting her to use the excuse that she's too plump and ungainly to scale the ladder, but she immediately sets about the task. And, in fact, she moves from rung to rung even more quickly than you probably could have done, soon reaching the very top of the signal. 'It's too dark to get much of a view from up here,' her distant voice carries down, 'but it was still worth the climb. There's something that could be a coded message scratched on the arm of the signal!'

Use the CODEBOOK CARD to find out what this message says by decoding the instruction below. If you don't have it in the KNAPSACK CARD, go to 183 instead.

158

Unfortunately, of course, you don't have the hijackers' codebook with you. If only Spooks had known this then he wouldn't have stopped behind and Miss Crumble would have been saved all that distress! You're all just about to start walking again when the lever for changing the points suddenly shifts position. Then something even scarier happens. There's a rumbling sound from the part of the track that branches off. It gradually grows louder and louder. 'You said there was probably an engine shed at the end of that branch line, didn't you, Professor?' you ask with a gulp. 'Do you think this could be the ghost train shunting out of it?' But the Professor is too petrified to give an answer. All your little group can do is peer along the line, anxiously waiting to see what's behind the rumbling . . . **Go to 76.**

159

'Come on, Professor!' Miss Crumble calls back to him impatiently, sure that his memory is not that short. 'You know that you don't have the map in your knapsack. It's just an excuse, isn't it, to delay joining us inside?' Strangely, though, there's no reply from the Professor. Worried about him, you and Miss Crumble immediately turn back to the door and step outside the shed again. You find the Professor with a stark white face and chattering teeth! It's a while before he can speak. 'I-I-I'm sure I saw the g-g-ghost train coming,' he stammers, pointing back along the line. 'There were these horrible sparks flying!' You and Miss Crumble peer along the line yourselves, into the darkness. There doesn't *appear* to be anything there. But wait a moment, what's that strange glow? It's getting brighter and brighter . . . **Go to 20.**

160

When you have recovered from this haunting, record it on the GHOST COUNTER. Now go to 248.

161

You now disappointedly lead the way back up the embankment, towards the railway line at the top. As you prepare to follow the line, you remember Mr Sporran saying that the hijacking took place at the last *station* before the bridge. That station must surely be shown on that map of his!

But did you bring Mr Sporran's MAP with you? If you did, use it to find which square the station is in – then follow the appropriate instruction below. If you don't have the MAP in your KNAPSACK CARD, you'll have to guess which instruction to follow.

If you think B3	go to 290
If you think A3	go to 317
If you think A4	go to 198

162

Fortunately, you're soon given an excuse to interrupt Miss Crumble's morbid talk. You spot a little wooden hut a short distance ahead, just to one side of the railway line. 'What do you think that was used for?' you ask, wondering if Mr Sporran's map would provide the answer.

Use the MAP to find which square the little wooden hut is in – then follow the appropriate instruction below. If you don't have the MAP in the KNAPSACK CARD, you'll have to guess which instruction to follow.

<pre>
        If you think C1   go to 313
        If you think D1   go to 125
        If you think E1   go to 263
</pre>

163

As Miss Crumble lifts her frowning face from the special dice, you know exactly what's coming. It's chosen *you* to take the lead through the carriage door. You ought to be a medium yourself! The others promise to keep right behind you as you now anxiously feel your way through the darkened carriage. You flash the Professor's torch on to the mouldy seats, to left and right, and up at the luggage rack. A small wooden chest suddenly appears in the beam. Could this contain the gold? You all lift it down, but when you try to open it, you find that it is firmly locked . . .

Do you have either of the KEYS in the KNAPSACK CARD? If

you do, place it exactly over the chest's lock below to see if it works – then follow the instruction. *(You may try both KEYS if you have them.)* If you don't have either of the *KEYS* – or your *KEY* doesn't work – go to **233** instead.

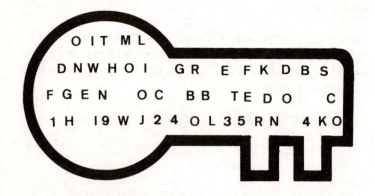

164

You haven't walked very far from the ruined church when you're sure you hear its bells faintly ring out behind you. 'It's nothing to get alarmed about,' the Professor calmly reassures you as you start to tremble. 'Remember, always look for the logical explanation first before assuming ghosts are at work. It's probably just this fierce wind that's rocking the bells.' But the Professor is soon trembling as much as you are, because you remind him that the church didn't have any bells. 'Don't you remember?' you ask him anxiously. 'The top part of the church was completely missing!' Has the ruined church suddenly come to life again, returning to the way it was in the old days? You all nervously look back at it . . . ***Go to 304.***

165

Disappointed at being able to unlock it, the Professor now warily steps through the carriage door. Even more warily, he leads you all along the dingy aisle, between the musty seats. You're hoping to find the bars of gold lying on one of the seats but there are just a few old yellowing newspapers there and a forgotten umbrella. But then Spooks suddenly spots something on the floor. It's another of the hijackers' codebooks! This proves that at least *they* came into this carriage even if their gold didn't!

If you don't already have it there, put the CODEBOOK into the KNAPSACK CARD. Now go to 134.

When you have recovered from this haunting, record it on the GHOST COUNTER. Now go to 34.

Thankfully, you were right! The tall white thing in the corner isn't anything . . . or at least anything you need worry about. It's just a stretcher, propped up against the wall. The Professor is so embarrassed by his display of nerves that he immediately gives you one of his little lectures to cover up. 'Yes, I expect there are quite a few stretchers stored away here,' he remarks brightly. 'They would have been ready in case anyone was badly injured in the mountains. Climbing can be a very dangerous business, you know.' Yes, and there's something else you know: the Professor is in the wrong profession; he's even more scared of ghosts than you are! **Go to 109.**

168

The damp, gloomy mist gets thicker and thicker as you all continue your exploration of the railway line, leaving the workmen's hut behind you. 'Keep as close to the track as possible, everyone!' Professor Bones urges from the front. 'If we wander too far away from it,' he adds nervously, 'we'll never find our way back again!' But that's exactly what the absent-minded Professor does, wanders too far from the track! And you, Miss Crumble and Spooks all stupidly follow him. You're lost! 'Really, Professor!' Miss Crumble chides him. 'Either those spectacles of yours need to be looked at or your head does. Which direction do we go *now* to try and find our way back to the railway line? I'll just have to consult my special dice . . .'

Throw the SPECIAL DICE – then turn to the appropriate paragraph number.

If ☠ thrown	go to 50
If 🦇 thrown	go to 139
If 👻 thrown	go to 223

169

Miss Crumble's special dice decides that *you* should be the one to lead you all into the mountain-rescue hut. You hesitate for a moment before putting your hand to the door, but then there's another fierce flash of lightning. If you wait outside much longer, someone might be struck! So you take a deep breath and turn the handle on the door. But the door refuses to open. It's obviously locked!

Do you have either of the KEYS in the KNAPSACK CARD? If you do, place it exactly over the door's 'lock' below to see if it works – then follow the instruction. (You may try both KEYS if you have them.) If you don't have either of the KEYS – or your KEY doesn't work – go to 55 instead.

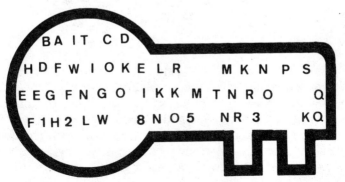

170

As soon as the padlock has clicked open, you all help to heave up the lid of the large grit box. The sight of what's inside leaves you all speechless. It's the gold, at least thirty gleaming bars of it! 'We've found it!' the Professor finally exclaims, doing a strange, joyful little dance. 'What a relief! We can all go home now!' Of course, it was really meant to be for the *ghosts* that the Professor and Miss Crumble had wanted to accompany you on this trip. But you're so delighted about the gold that you decide not to embarrass them. You just give Spooks a little wink!

Well done! But don't forget that there is more than one stack of gold hidden near the railway line. If you would like to attempt to find the others as well, you must start the exploration again from the beginning. Try setting off with a different ITEM this time.

171

You have to remind the Professor that, unfortunately, you *didn't* borrow the codebook. 'Oh no, so we didn't!' he remembers, scratching his absent-minded head. 'What a pity,' he adds, 'what a pity!' A moment later, you all suddenly freeze on the spot. There's a clonking noise way above you. Someone is walking across the rickety bridge! 'P-p-perhaps it's the g-g-ghost of one of those h-h-hijackers,' the Professor stammers, not daring to look up. 'Perhaps his poor soul walks up and down the bridge,' he continues, 'making sure other trains don't use it.' You are sure there's a more logical explanation for the noise, however. It's probably just one of those shaggy Highland cows gone astray and investigating the bridge. So you slowly lift your head to check . . . **Go to 130.**

172

When you have recovered from this haunting, record it on the GHOST COUNTER. Now go to 107.

173

Frustrated and annoyed about the locked box, Miss Crumble looks all round the dusty floor. 'Perhaps there's something in here we can use to force it open,' she suggests. She then notices that Professor Bones is still eagerly examining some of the levers. 'And perhaps you could help us, Professor?' she suggests rather sharply, putting her hands on her hips. 'We've come here to try and find the gold, you know, not to look at railway curios!' As the Professor apologetically joins in your search, you suddenly hear something coming up the wooden steps outside. It's something with a very light tread. Could it be a ghost? you wonder, as you all wait quivering for it to appear . . . **Go to 123.**

174

'Oh, silly me!' exclaims the Professor as you eagerly reach into his knapsack for the codebook Mr Sporran had lent you. 'I forgot that I had that with me. And here was I trying to decipher this complicated-looking message without a single clue. What does it work out as?' But you're only prepared to tell him once he has led you all inside the eerie cottage. So the Professor pushes the gnarled wooden door and tensely steps through. He can wait not a second longer, excitedly rubbing his bony hands together. 'The message was obviously written by one of the hijackers,' you tell him, relieving his suspense. 'But a hijacker with an irritating sense of humour. It says that the gold might be hidden in the cottage or it might not!' **Go to 252.**

175
It just isn't Miss Crumble's day. Her special dice again decides that *she* should take the lead! When she finally reaches the dilapidated signal box, she asks you and the Professor if you would like her to lead the way up the little wooden steps as well. 'If you would prefer, I can always throw my special dice again,' she suggests. But she can

tell by your faces that she is being far too hopeful, and she reluctantly starts to mount the steps. The rotting wood creaks and groans under her weight. She's just about to nudge open the flapping door at the top when she notices that some strange symbols have been chiselled into it. Was this the work of one of the hijackers?

Do you have the CODEBOOK in the KNAPSACK CARD? If you do, use it to find out what the message says by decoding the instruction below. If you don't, go to 201 instead.

176

The Professor is just about to record this haunting on his ghost counter, however, when Miss Crumble stops him. 'That glow is not a ghost train, Professor,' she tells him, lifting her glasses to her eyes and peering through them. 'It's nowhere near the railway line; it's coming from half-way up that mountain over there. I've never known a railway line run up a steep mountain! It must be the light from a farmer's bonfire.' The Professor peers through his own glasses, eventually admitting that Miss Crumble is right. 'What a shame!' he says with a tut. 'I so much *wanted* that to be the ghost train!' You can't help smiling secretly to yourself. The Professor might not have a nerve for ghosts, but he certainly does for lying! **Go to 270.**

177

Your group nervously makes its way back up the embankment so you can explore the railway line now. You can't resist turning your head one last time, though, to look at the fast-flowing river way below the bridge. Black, misty and deep, it's the gloomiest river you've ever seen. 'I wonder if they ever found the bodies,' Miss Crumble says quite cheerfully as you start to follow the abandoned railway line away from the bridge, then adds, 'or perhaps they're still lying there, right at the bottom!' **Go to 162.**

178

When you have recovered from this haunting, record it on the GHOST COUNTER. Now go to 66.

179

You all become more and more excited as word by word you decode the message on the door. It works out as: *GOLD HIDDEN INSIDE THIS HUT*! But as Miss Crumble now leads you all inside the dark little building she warns you against being too expectant. 'It might just be a mean trick of the hijackers,' she says. 'We know that they weren't very nice people. They seemed rather horrid little men!' It's really difficult to contain your excitement, though, especially when Spooks discovers a large orange key on the floor of the hut. Is this to open the chest containing the gold?

If you don't already have it there, put the ORANGE KEY into the KNAPSACK CARD. Now go to 109.

180

Miss Crumble points out that you didn't bring the map. You're fully aware of this, of course. You had mentioned it merely to distract Miss Crumble and the Professor from their bickering! But it doesn't work because they soon start arguing again. They're like two little children! 'To a scientist, Miss Crumble,' the Professor starts up pompously, 'that special dice of yours is just a load of nonsense. We only believe in things that –' But his voice suddenly breaks off as you all hear an eerie wailing sound from way above you. It seems to be coming from the direction of that stone tower on the hill. You all nervously lift your eyes towards it . . . **Go to 48.**

181

Miss Crumble is not the only one with premonitions. For, just as you had feared, the special dice decides that *you* should be the one to go and investigate the eerie cottage. Deciding that putting it off will only make your nerves worse, you immediately set off through the mist. You're soon approaching the little wooden door at the front and your careful footsteps seem to grow slower and slower. You wonder if the cottage's last owner had ever seen the ghost train . . . and gone stark staring mad! At last you reach the door but (not sure whether you're pleased by this or not), you find that it is locked.

Do you have either of the KEYS in the KNAPSACK CARD? If you do, place it exactly over the door's 'lock' below to see if it works – then follow the instruction. If you don't have either of the KEYS – or your KEY doesn't work – go to 327 instead.

182

The church door creaks loudly as you push it open. First Miss Crumble passes through, then the Professor, then you and then . . . Well, it ought to be Spooks, but he's not there! 'Spooks!' Miss Crumble cries out anxiously into the night. 'Where are you?' The Professor slowly shines his torch around, lighting up the overgrown graveyard and the eerie trees beyond. Suddenly something small and white appears in the beam. Is it Spooks or is it a tiny ghost? It's Spooks! Tired of looking for the gold, he must have gone searching for rabbits instead! ***Go to 257.***

183

Unfortunately, of course, you don't have the codebook with you. Even if you had, neither you nor the Professor would have been that happy about taking it up to Miss Crumble. You're sure that the rusty ladder can only just about sustain her ample weight, let alone yours as well! As you're waiting for Miss Crumble to come back down from the top of the signal, Spooks suddenly starts to growl. It's a deep, nervous growl; his twitching nose seems to sense something further along the track. Looking that direction yourself, you think that you can just about make out a red light swaying from side to side. You remember that track workers sometimes used to swing a red light to warn the train to stop. Could this be the *ghost* of one of those men? ***Go to 315.***

184

When you have recovered from this haunting, record it on the GHOST COUNTER. Now go to 94.

185

You're just thinking about climbing *over* the locomotive's door – squeezing yourself through the little open window above it – when you hear a crunching noise. It appears to be coming from the rear of the locomotive, where the coal is kept. Is something crawling over the coal? A rat, perhaps? But if it is a rat, you're sure that Spooks would have leapt in after it. He loves chasing rats. Spooks is frozen to the spot, though, looking quite terrified! Could it be a ghost sitting amongst the coal? You all nervously retreat from the locomotive, wondering if something is suddenly going to jump up from it . . . **Go to 106.**

186

The Professor's relief soon turns to anxiety again as the huge steel door now responds to his tug on the handle. It slowly creaks open. There's soon a wide enough gap for you all to squeeze through, but the Professor insists on pulling the folding door back as far as possible. He seems to have *two* reasons for this. First, to let in as much as possible of the little light that's left in the sky. And second, to enable you all to make a swift escape if necessary! He can at last pull back the door no further and he tentatively leads your little group into the vast shed. Your heart freezes as you notice that there are two old carriages inside, and a rusty, spooky-looking locomotive! ***Go to 51.***

187

When you have recovered from this haunting, record it on the GHOST COUNTER. Now go to 18.

188

In some ways, you're rather glad that you can't open the tomb. Imagine if the Professor was wrong about it being a secret hiding-place and you found a dry old skeleton inside! Even if he was right, it seems unlikely that the hijackers would have known about it. So as you now leave the graveyard, you're not too disappointed. You haven't left the church far behind when you hear a rattling sound coming from that direction. Is it the ghost of one of the hijackers? Perhaps some of them had been buried in that graveyard! You all nervously turn your heads to find out . . . ***Go to 24.***

189

Miss Crumble now leads the way into the station, hesitantly shining the Professor's torch in front of her. There are cobwebs everywhere! The torch beam moves from one dark object to another: a rusty luggage trolley . . . the cracked ticket window . . . a timetable peeling off the wall . . . someone's face! Miss Crumble immediately drops the torch in fright. But you calmly pick it up again. 'It's just an old weighing-machine,' you say with a gentle chuckle as you direct the torch beam back into that corner. 'Take a look, Miss Crumble. What you thought was a face is just the circular glass part that displays your weight!' ***Go to 248.***

190

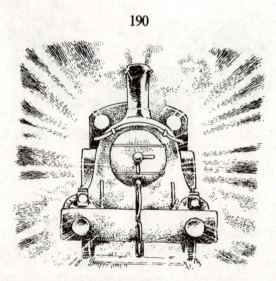

When you have recovered from this haunting, record it on the GHOST COUNTER. Now go to 46.

191

Having thrown back the lid of the chest, you all eagerly look inside. But it's completely empty! 'We should have known that the gold wouldn't have been left in a place as obvious as this,' you remark disappointedly. 'This empty chest must be a little practical joke of the hijackers!' But perhaps unlocking the chest wasn't a complete waste of time. Miss Crumble suddenly notices a folded sheet of paper lying at the bottom, under a thick layer of dust. It's a map of the railway line.

If you don't already have it there, put the MAP into the KNAPSACK CARD. Now go to 69.

192

You and the Professor hold your breath as Miss Crumble slowly lifts her head from the special dice. Whom has it decided should lead the way to the bridge? 'I'm sorry, Professor Bones,' she announces gravely, 'but I'm afraid my special dice has chosen you!' The Professor turns quite white at her announcement but then manages to put a brave face on it. 'I was hoping it would be me,' he says, somewhat untruthfully, as he starts to stride towards the eerie bridge. But as the wrecked bridge comes nearer and nearer through the hanging mist, clearer and clearer, his courage deserts him again. 'Perhaps we should make absolutely sure we've got the right one before we go any further,' he suggests rather slyly. 'Let's see what the bridge looks like on the map.'

Do you have the MAP in the KNAPSACK CARD? If you do, use it to find which square the railway bridge is in – then follow the appropriate instruction below. If you don't have the MAP, you'll have to guess which instruction to follow.

      If you think E1   go to 85
      If you think D1   go to 326
      If you think E2   go to 234

193

You now leave the eerie bridge behind you, starting to follow the railway line away from it. You haven't walked very far when you come across a small wooden hut at the edge of the track. 'It looks like a shelter for the labourers who worked on the line,' the Professor remarks, fascinated. 'Or perhaps it's where they stored their tools. You know, I'm just having a thought . . .' But you and Miss Crumble have already had the same thought ahead of him. At least, you assume it's the same thought – perhaps there are not only workmen's tools lying in that hut but also one of the crates of gold! While the Professor is still scratching his head, deep in thought, you and Miss Crumble rush to the door of the hut. Unfortunately, it's locked! This looks like a job for one of those two keys again . . .

Do you have either of the KEYS in the KNAPSACK CARD? If

you do, place it exactly over the hut door's 'lock' below to see if it works – then follow the instruction. If you don't have either of the KEYS – or your KEY doesn't work – go to 239 instead.

194

You haven't walked much further along the main branch of the railway line when you reach an old signal. 'I bet there's quite a good view from the top,' the Professor remarks as he stares up the rusty ladder. He peers at you through his little round spectacles. 'Why don't you climb up,' he suggests, 'and see if there's a station further along the line?' But you're rather reluctant to do this, finding the signal quite eerie. You're sure the striped arm at the top is about to move at any moment! Miss Crumble sympathises with you and asks the Professor why *he* doesn't climb the ladder since it's his idea. 'But we'll be completely fair about this,' she adds. 'I'll let my special dice decide who should go up.'

Throw the SPECIAL DICE – then turn to the appropriate number.

If ☠ thrown	go to 126
If 🦇 thrown	go to 157
If 👻 thrown	go to 49

195

Unfortunately, of course, you decided not to borrow the hijackers' codebook from the museum. But it would have made little difference if you had, for the bridge suddenly starts to sway beneath you; it's about to give way! 'Quick, hurry back to the bank!' you frantically shout to the others. You only just make it – there's an almighty crash right behind you. 'Do you think that was the work of one of the hijackers' ghosts?' you ask, shaking all over, not daring to turn round. The ghost might still be there, hovering above the wreckage! But you're going to have to turn your heads eventually, so you slowly and anxiously glance over your shoulders . . . **Go to 86.**

196

'It's the face of Florence Sullivan staring through the window, isn't it?' Miss Crumble gasps weakly as she nearly faints into the Professor's arms. You quickly help him support her heavy weight, holding one of her elbows. 'No, it was your *own* face you saw in the window, Miss Crumble,' you say, soothing her with a kindly chuckle. 'It's so dark outside the carriage, and with the torch lighting you up so brightly, your face made a strong reflection. Look, you can see *my* face in the window now. And if I lifted Spooks up and shone the torch on him, you would see *his* as well!' **Go to 134.**

197

The way the Professor's eyes suddenly light up shows that he has finished decoding the message on the level-crossing gates. But he is so absent-minded that he forgets to tell you and Miss Crumble what it works out as! 'Oh, do forgive me, Miss Crumble,' he hums dreamily as she sternly reminds him of your presence. 'The message says that we are to search round the foot of this gatepost. I wouldn't be at all surprised if that's where one of the chests of gold is buried!' No sooner has the Professor told you this than Miss Crumble instructs Spooks to start digging. The eager little dog doesn't uncover any gold, unfortunately, but he does scoop out a large green key!

If you don't already have it there, put the GREEN KEY into the KNAPSACK CARD. Now go to 34.

198

Your little group now starts to follow the abandoned railway line. There's an eerie quietness about it, weeds growing up between the rotting sleepers. 'Look how rusty the rails are,' Professor Bones observes, 'no shine on them at all. Surely that proves that these rumours of a ghost train are mere poppycock? I'm afraid this visit of ours looks like being a complete waste of time!' But you can tell that the Professor isn't as convinced by his deduction as he pretends. Certainly, he's right about the rails. They don't have any shine to them. This would prove that it had been a very long time since an ordinary train had used them . . . but of course a ghost train *isn't* an ordinary train. Maybe it doesn't leave any evidence of its journeys! ***Go to 127.***

199

'I'm afraid, dear child,' Miss Crumble informs you gravely, 'that the special dice has elected *you* to lead us into the tunnel. But don't worry, Spooks can go with you at the front!' Spooks doesn't seem at all happy about this, though. Whenever Miss Crumble goes first he has to accompany her, and now that you are to go first, he has to accompany *you*! The little dog seems to go into a sulk, trotting off towards the side of the tunnel. 'Now come back here, Spooks!' Miss Crumble orders him sternly. 'You know I won't tolerate that sort of behaviour!' But then she realises that she has misjudged him. Spooks had trotted off towards the side of the tunnel because he had noticed some symbols chiselled there!

*Use the **CODEBOOK** to find out what this message says by decoding the instruction below. If you don't have the **CODE-BOOK** in the **KNAPSACK CARD**, go to 242 instead.*

200

You cautiously nudge open the cottage door and step inside. 'Anyone there?' you call out hoarsely, but of course you know that there won't be. Not mortals at any rate! The inside is even more eerie than you were expecting, huge sheets of cobwebs trailing from ceiling to floor. They cling to your face as you pass from the tiny bare living-room to the even tinier and barer bedroom. Apart from the bed itself, the only thing in there is a small chest of drawers. You quickly check through the drawers just in case some of the gold has been transferred there. There's no gold, but hidden away at the back of the bottom drawer is a large green key!

If you don't already have it there, put the GREEN KEY into the KNAPSACK CARD. Now go to 35.

201

Since you're unable to decode the message on the door, Miss Crumble cautiously leads the way through it. Inside, it seems to be full of rusty handles and levers covered with trailing cobwebs. The Professor strides over to one of the levers and tugs at it. 'How marvellous!' he says enthusiastically. 'These were for operating the signals. The red ones would be for the stop signals and the green ones for . . .' But his voice trails off. One of the levers starts to make a loud grinding noise, as if something is moving it! You all rush for the door and it's only when you're safely outside that you dare look back at the signal box. You slowly lift your eyes towards its windows . . . ***Go to 87.***

202

When you have recovered from this haunting, record it on the GHOST COUNTER. Now go to 168.

203

'I can't see anything sitting there, can you?' the Professor whispers, breathing heavily, as you all nervously stare at the stove. The tin mug starts to rattle again on the surface. 'It must be one of the invisible types of ghosts!' he shrieks. You all nearly jump out of your skins as the tin mug suddenly drops to the floor! But then you give a huge sigh of relief, and you can't help laughing when a little mouse crawls out. The Professor joins in, letting out a strange, high-pitched chuckle. And so does Spooks, jovially wagging his tail. The only one who doesn't feel your relief is Miss Crumble. She gives a terrified scream instead. As you step outside the hut you remember that she can't stand the sight of mice! **Go to 168.**

204

You now have to decide in which direction to follow the farm track. Do you follow it to the north or to the south? Miss Crumble suddenly starts to sway, closing her eyes. 'I think I'm receiving one of my messages from beyond,' she announces in that eerie chant of hers. 'It says to let Spooks decide the direction!' Her little dog puts his nose to the ground and has a good sniff. Then he chooses the track on the south side of the level crossing. But as you all start to follow him, you rather wonder about the reason for Spooks's choice. Is it because he thinks the gold is in this direction? Or is it because he thinks this is the quickest way home! **Go to 34.**

205

Your little group now nervously explores the vast interior of the engine shed. Two old carriages and then a rusty locomotive suddenly appear in the beam of your torch. It's probably very similar to the one that plunged off the bridge – the ghost train – but, fortunately, this one is real. You gingerly touch its wheels and then its buffers at the front; they're quite solid. You decide to climb up into the locomotive, mounting the little iron steps. But when you tug the rusty door, you find that it's locked. You're sure one of those two keys will open it. But which?

Do you have either of the KEYS in the KNAPSACK CARD? If you do, place it exactly over the locomotive door's 'lock' below – then follow the instruction. (You may try both KEYS if you have them.) If you don't have either of the KEYS – or your KEY doesn't work – go to 185 instead.

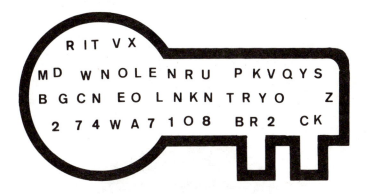

206

'Let's all give the larder door a really good tug and see if we can force it open,' you suggest to the others. 'It might just be that the gold's hidden inside!' But then you suddenly notice an old calendar on the wall, for the year 1911. This proves that the cottage was inhabited for some years after the train robbery. Surely the hijackers would only have hidden their gold there if the cottage had been abandoned completely? So it looks as if you can forget about not only the larder but also every other possible hiding-place there. It's with considerable relief that you all step outside again. But then you hear a furious tapping just behind you, from one of the cottage's broken windows. Is this the owner's ghost, incensed by your intrusion? You all nervously peer over your shoulders to find out . . . ***Go to 122.***

207

Miss Crumble's special dice decides that *you* should be the one to guess the direction for the railway line. 'I'm sure you'll get it right, dear,' she tells you. 'If the special dice has chosen you, then it must be because it thinks you have the best chance!' Not totally convinced by this, you nevertheless agree to take the responsibility. You're just about to choose a direction when the Professor suggests locating this loch on Mr Sporran's map. 'We did borrow the map, didn't we?' he asks, scratching his head.

Use the MAP to find which square the loch (a narrow lake) is in – then follow the appropriate instruction. If you don't have the MAP in the KNAPSACK CARD, you'll have to guess which instruction to follow.

> If you think D2   go to 297
> If you think E2   go to 100
> If you think E3   go to 281

208

When you have recovered from this haunting, record it on the GHOST COUNTER. Now go to 252.

209

But, of course, you don't have the map with you. It's unfortunate because that needle of rock might well have helped you find your way again. As you all continue *guessing* a route through the mist, Miss Crumble can't help poking fun at the Professor. 'A huge ghostly figure indeed, Professor Bones!' she mocks. 'I think you'd better let me give those spectacles a good polish for you!' Rather to the Professor's annoyance, even Spooks seems to join in the teasing, happily wagging his tail. But then the wagging suddenly stops, and so does Miss Crumble's laughter. There's a piercing cry from behind you, roughly where that needle of rock is. Perhaps Professor Bones was right about it being a ghost, after all! ***Go to 71.***

210

On turning your head, you find that it's just a wild deer that's been following you. You're about to tell the Professor and Miss Crumble, who are still too frightened to look round, but you decide to teach them a lesson instead. 'Yes, it is a g-g-ghost!' you stammer, frozen to the spot. 'And it won't go away. W-w-what do we do? You two are the experts on ghosts.' But they're still both unable to speak and the only one who dares to look back is Spooks. On spotting the deer, he swaps a little grin with you. Perhaps it's now time to relieve the other two of their misery! ***Go to 66.***

211

Your little group now leaves the ruined church, deciding to continue further along this route, away from the railway line. The hijackers might have wanted to hide the gold as far from the track as possible. 'We should certainly try a bit further,' the Professor recommends, 'although obviously there wouldn't have been time for them to carry the gold too many miles. I wonder how many miles we have come already?' There's a very easy way of finding out, of course. That is to locate the church on Mr Sporran's map.

But do you have the MAP with you? If you do, use it to find which square the church is in – then follow the instruction. If you don't, you'll have to guess which instruction to follow.

<blockquote>
If you think A3   go to 164
If you think B3   go to 138
If you think B4   go to 18
</blockquote>

212

'I suppose we had better quickly search the castle, hadn't we?' you suggest tentatively as you walk right up to its dark, sombre walls. You certainly don't relish the idea, but it does seem an ideal hiding-place. So you all nervously pass through the main entrance, wondering if any horrible murders or massacres ever occurred within these walls. It seems an ideal place for *those* as well! Fortunately, there's so little of the ancient castle still standing that your search is soon completed. But *unfortunately*, there's absolutely no sign of the gold in there! **Go to 39.**

213

'What a pity we don't have the means to unlock it,' the Professor remarks as he tries in vain to open the collection box without a key. 'I don't think any of the gold is hidden inside. There isn't enough room. But I was hoping that the hijackers might have dropped some sort of clue through the slot for the coins, a map or a scribbled note.' You are just about to suggest that you try turning the collection box upside down and giving it a good shake when you hear a noise from the tiny choir-stall above. Something is moving about up there . . . **Go to 75.**

214

When you have recovered from this haunting, record it on the GHOST COUNTER. Now go to 323.

215

As the Professor and Miss Crumble investigate the animal shelter, checking that some of the gold hasn't been hidden amongst the crumbling lumps of stone, you look down into the valley over to your left. You're sure this is the valley through which the railway line runs. It's now so dark, though, that it's impossible to make out the track. Suddenly you spot a faint glow moving along the valley. Petrified, you wonder if this is the ghost train making one of its journeys. The next moment something rises from the glow and floats through the dark sky towards you! **Go to 187.**

216

Miss Crumble keeps tugging the handle on the trap-door, hoping to open it even without the key. 'Be careful, won't you, Miss Crumble?' you tell her rather anxiously as she is showered with dust and cobwebs, 'we don't want to bring the whole ceiling down!' So she finally gives up, letting out a long sigh. 'Well, I'm sure there's only more rescue equipment up there,' she remarks wearily. 'I certainly don't think we're going to be finding that gold today anyway. Not here or anywhere else, I'm afraid. I would be receiving one of my special messages if we were. But I'm not getting a single thing!' You and the Professor don't normally believe in Miss Crumble's 'messages'. But you've got the same pessimistic feeling about this particular exploration yourselves. So you decide to abort your search for the time being, and make the long trek back to Coldhaggis. You all hope you won't be too late to find a nice warm bed somewhere!

If you would like another attempt at finding the hijackers' gold, you must start the game again from the beginning. Try setting off with a different ITEM this time to see if it gives you more luck.

217

Miss Crumble's slight gulp as she glances down at her special dice shows that it must have chosen *her* to lead the way into the hut. She's just about to nudge open the door, however, when she notices that there is something else written there. Just below *Mountain-Rescue Hut* there are some more faded letters; these are much less neat, as if they had been quickly scribbled. 'Wait a minute!' she exclaims as she lifts her spectacles to her nose to examine the letters more closely. 'They're not letters at all, but symbols. This is obviously some sort of coded message!'

Use the CODEBOOK CARD to find out what this message says

by decoding the instruction below. If you don't have the CODEBOOK in your KNAPSACK CARD, go to 255 instead.

218
Since you're unable to open the door on the locomotive's boiler, you're just going to have to hope that the gold isn't in there. 'The padlock was probably just for safety reasons,' the Professor remarks, trying to reassure you all, 'so that cats or other animals didn't hide away in there. They would have been roasted otherwise!' You all now step down from the locomotive so you can investigate one of the carriages. But you've only just turned your back on it when there's a clatter of metal. It sounds like one of the rusty shovels that you'd noticed propped up against the boiler. But why is it suddenly clattering? Has someone knocked it over? 'P-p-perhaps it's the g-g-ghost of one of the b-b-boilermen!' Miss Crumble stammers as you all slowly look round . . . **Go to 113.**

219
As the Professor decodes the message of the front of the locomotive, his expression becomes more and more excited. You're sure his eyes are suddenly going to pop out through his glasses! This is all too

much for you and Miss Crumble to bear and she insists that the Professor immediately reveal what he has decoded. Even Spooks seems to want to know, starting to yap at him. 'Very well, very well!' the Professor replies eagerly. 'This is what the message says. Are you ready? It says that the gold is hidden somewhere inside the engine shed!' Is your search about to come to an end at last you all wonder, hopefully, or is the message just a mean joke of the hijackers? ***Go to 46.***

220

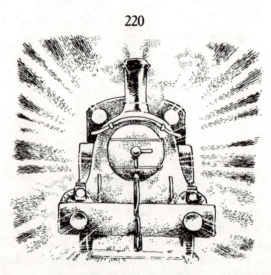

When you have recovered from this haunting, record it on the GHOST COUNTER. (Don't forget: when you have recorded four hauntings, you must immediately stop the adventure and start the game all over again.) Now go to 257.

221

You're all just about to leave the water tank when the Professor suddenly has another idea. This is an even better one! 'Of course, we're all assuming that there's still just water in the tank,' he exclaims, his eyebrows suddenly jumping above his spectacles. 'But perhaps it's the gold in there. Have any of you considered that?' So you quickly scramble up the side of the tank and lift back the protective cover on the top. Well, the Professor was right. There *isn't* any water in there any more. But, unfortunately, the gold isn't there either! The tank isn't completely empty, though, for lying on the dry, rusty bottom is a large orange key!

If you don't already have it there, put the ORANGE KEY into the KNAPSACK CARD. Now go to 94.

222

Miss Crumble's special dice decides that the Professor should lead the exploration of the carriage. So he tries to convince himself that he is not in the least nervous about it after all. He rubs his bony hands together with a pretended glee. 'I've never seen a ghost sitting in a train carriage before!' he remarks. 'This will be a first for me. I just can't wait until I announce it to the other ghost experts at our next conference. They're going to be so envious!' This false glee of his is soon replaced by a genuine one, however. For when the Professor tries to open the door to the carriage, he finds that it is securely locked!

Do you have either of the KEYS in the KNAPSACK CARD? If you do, place it exactly over the carriage door's 'lock' below to see if it works – then follow the instruction. (You may try both KEYS if you have them.) If you don't have either of the KEYS – or your KEY doesn't work – go to 254 instead.

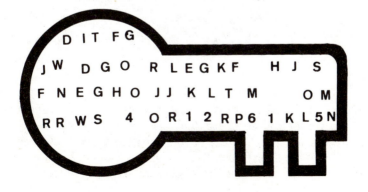

223

Miss Crumble's special dice apparently advises you to walk off to your right to find the railway line again. You use the word 'apparently' because you're still not sure whether you really believe in the dice. You believe in it even less when you've hiked a good couple of miles or so in this direction and still haven't come back to the railway line! 'Oh my gosh!' the Professor suddenly exclaims, his thin body starting to tremble . . . **Go to 21.**

224

'It's *you* I'm afraid, Professor Bones!' Miss Crumble announces as she studies her special dice. His thin body shivers but then he bravely leads the way towards the tunnel entrance. 'We can't go in too far,' he says nervously over his shoulder, 'or we won't be able to see a thing. I'd suggest just a hundred metres or so.' The Professor has walked about fifty metres, his nervous footsteps echoing eerily round the tunnel, when he suddenly stops . . . **Go to 133.**

225

'Miss Crumble, look out!' you suddenly shout at her as she leans her heavy weight against the handrail. She just about jumps back in time. The wooden handrail is so rotten that it snaps clean away and crashes to the floor below. As she puts her hand to her heart in shock, you all hear what sounds like a faint sniggering above you. Is it some sort of ghost meanly laughing at Miss Crumble's near accident, or is it just a bird cooing away? You all anxiously lift your heads to check . . . **Go to 112.**

226

When you have recovered from this haunting, record it on the GHOST COUNTER. Now go to 248.

227

You try not to be too disappointed about the locked door and suggest shining your torch through the little cracked window instead. 'Perhaps that will be enough to show us if there's anything inside the ticket office,' you remark. So you jam your torch into the little hole where the money and tickets were passed through and shine it round as far as you can. You're just about to tell the others that you can only see a couple of old chairs in there when the dark hall is suddenly filled by a strange glow. The glow's source seems to be outside, from the direction of the platform! Does that mean that the ghost train is slowly passing through? You all nervously turn round and peer out at the quiet platform . . . **Go to 30.**

228

Having reached the top of the ladder, you shine the Professor's torch along the thick iron girders up there. These are for supporting the shed's roof, but does one of them also support the bars of gold? 'Any luck?' the Professor calls up eagerly from the bottom of the ladder. 'Have you spotted them yet?' You're just about to shake your head disappointedly at him when your torch beam reaches a junction where three of the girders join. Resting on this much wider part is a stack of gleaming yellow bars! In your delight, you almost topple from the ladder. You've at last found the hijackers' gold!

Well done! But don't forget that there is more than one stack of gold hidden near the railway line. If you would like to attempt to find the others as well you must start your exploration again from the beginning. Try setting off with a different ITEM this time.

229

As Miss Crumble studies the roll of her special dice, her face first goes pale then quickly turns an excited pink. You can guess what this means. It means that the dice has chosen *her* to lead towards the bridge, but she's trying to pretend she doesn't mind! 'Come on, Spooks!' she calls as she waddles purposefully towards the bridge. 'If we're really lucky,' she tells him, 'we might see some ghosts sitting there!' Like you, Spooks is very relieved to find that there *aren't* any ghosts on the bridge, but it's still a very forbidding construction. A dangerous one, too! 'Don't go too far along it, Miss Crumble,' you warn her anxiously, 'we don't know how safe it is.' But Miss Crumble leads you further and further along the rickety bridge, nearer and nearer to where it suddenly ends... **Go to 329.**

230

Of course, Miss Crumble has forgotten that you didn't bring the map from the museum with you. But her forgetfulness is perfectly understandable under the circumstances. The poor thing seems a bag of nerves! Nevertheless, she now leads the way into the station, stepping inside the dark hall. She nervously shines the Professor's torch round and the beam suddenly lights up several old timetables which are peeling off the wall. Fascinated, the Professor walks over to study one of these. Peering through his little glasses, he's just about to read out the timetable's year when you hear a high-pitched noise outside. It sounds like a guard's whistle! You all tensely peer out of the nearest window, towards the platform . . . ***Go to 160.***

231

As you look out over the mist-shrouded loch, you all seem to be having exactly the same thought. This one might not be Loch Ness but it's not very far from it. And what do you associate with Loch Ness? A monster! 'You don't think there might be a monster lurking in here as well, do you, Professor?' you ask anxiously. But the Professor really doesn't know, reminding you that his area of expertise is ghosts – not monsters! 'I do know one thing, though,' he adds with a gulp, 'I think we should walk away from this loch as quickly as possible. Not because I find it scary at all. Indeed, I find it most fascinating. But if we're going to investigate this ghost train properly we must get back to the railway line.' So who is going to try and find the way there this time? Miss Crumble suggests letting her special dice decide.

Throw the SPECIAL DICE – then turn to the appropriate number.

If 💀 thrown		go to 318
If 🦇 thrown		go to 79
If 👻 thrown		go to 207

232

When you have recovered from this haunting, record it on the GHOST COUNTER. Now go to 109.

233

Since you're unable to open the little chest, you give it a quick shake to find out what the contents sound like. It's certainly not bars of gold! They would have made a heavy, thudding sound, but this is more like shoes tumbling about. The chest must have belonged to one of the train's passengers, containing his or her clothes. This seems to be confirmed when you turn the chest over because the name *Florence Sullivan* is engraved on the bottom. Miss Crumble suddenly starts to look rather strange, taking the torch from you. 'I'm sure Florence Sullivan is very close by at this moment,' she whispers slowly and very eerily, 'I can feel her presence really strongly!' As Miss Crumble stands up to look out of the carriage window, she suddenly lets out a piercing scream . . . ***Go to 196.***

234

But you know full well that this is just a ploy of the Professor's to delay reaching the bridge. He'd tried that trick more than once at Ghostly Towers! 'Of course it's the right bridge, Professor,' you tell

him gently but firmly. 'I doubt that there are many collapsed railway bridges in this area. Besides, if you remember, we didn't bring the map with us. We borrowed one of the other items from the museum.' So the Professor has no choice but to continue towards the black, eerie-looking bridge. He's led you all only a few steps nearer, however, when he suddenly stops dead in his tracks. 'What's that loud whistling noise?' he asks, his huge, terrified eyes nearly popping through his spectacles. 'Is it the ghost train already?'
Go to 56.

235

'You will be careful going down that embankment, won't you, Professor Bones?' Miss Crumble warns him. 'It might be very slippery.' The Professor assumes from this warning that her special dice had chosen *him* to go first! Although he does start to climb down, it's not without a little complaining. 'You know, I just wonder how *scientific* that dice of yours is, Miss Crumble,' he remarks as he carefully descends the bank. 'I have to say, it's not something that I personally would have faith in.' But his complaints suddenly cease as he reaches one of the stout iron supports for the bridge. 'Good heavens!' he excitedly exclaims. 'Look here! I do believe there's some sort of coded message scratched into the metal. We did borrow that codebook from Mr Sporran's museum, didn't we?'

Did you? If you did, use it to find out what the message says by decoding the instruction below. If you don't have the CODEBOOK in your KNAPSACK CARD, go to 171 instead.

236

Since you're unable to decode the message on the level-crossing gates, you now start to follow the farm track. 'We'll see if it leads to a deserted farmhouse or something,' you remark as you walk. 'But we'll only give it a mile or so. If we don't spot a likely hiding-place by then, we'll make our way back to the railway line.' The railway line still isn't far behind, however, when you hear the level-crossing gates suddenly slam shut. Was it merely that the wind has grown strong enough to blow them shut, or did the gates shut by themselves, perhaps because the ghost train is approaching along the line? You all nervously turn round, wondering if the train will suddenly appear . . . ***Go to 89.***

237

'Ah, just as I was hoping!' Miss Crumble pretends outrageously, rubbing her chubby hands together, as she studies the roll of her special dice. 'It's chosen *me* to go and investigate the cottage. I wonder how many ghosts there will be!' As she confidently waddles off into the mist (although you notice Spooks has been made to accompany her) the Professor suggests looking for the cottage on Mr Sporran's map. 'It will show us exactly where we are,' he says as if it's the most brilliant idea ever.

Do you have the MAP in the KNAPSACK CARD? If you do, use it to find which square the crofter's cottage is in – then follow the appropriate instruction. If you don't, you'll have to guess which instruction to follow.

If you think D3	go to 58
If you think E2	go to 275
If you think E3	go to 324

238

When you have recovered from this haunting, record it on the GHOST COUNTER. Now go to 17.

239

'Perhaps if we give the door a really good pull, it will open without a key,' you say, to console everyone. Then you get them to help you but, although it creaks a little, the door remains firmly fastened. 'Well, we've got to get into the hut somehow,' you insist, walking round to the back. 'Hey! How about here? There's an open window behind this shutter. It's not big enough for any of *us* to climb through, but Spooks should have no problem!' So you all lift a rather reluctant Spooks up to the window, and the little dog jumps through and starts to search round the hut. A few minutes later his furry head reappears. He looks disappointed. 'No gold in there, my little dear?' Miss Crumble assumes as she lifts him out again. 'Never mind,' she adds, 'you did your best!' Your little group now leaves the hut but it's not far behind you when you hear that wooden shutter suddenly fly open again, making a loud clatter. Was it just a sudden gust of wind that caused this, or has Spooks disturbed a ghost? **Go to 276.**

240

You give the firm padlock an irritated shake. If only you had the right key with you! But all is not lost because there's another way of getting into the coal-yard; by clambering over the wall! You all help each other, Miss Crumble proving surprisingly agile at this sort of thing. You're sure she must have been a cat-burglar or something similar in her youth! Unfortunately, though, your efforts are all in vain. The only thing in the coal-yard is . . . coal. You have all just clambered out again and dropped the short distance to the ground, when you hear a strange howling inside the yard. Did you disturb a stray dog sleeping in there? Or was it a *ghost* you disturbed? You all tensely lift your heads to see if anything appears at the top of the wall . . . **Go to 214.**

241

You now reach the signal box, the Professor nervously leading the way up the little wooden steps at its side. 'It's all right, Professor,' Miss Crumble whispers as he hesitates by the flapping, rotten door at the top, 'I can't *sense* any ghosts in there.' But this is of little comfort to him. When Miss Crumble does sense ghosts, there usually aren't any . . . and so when she doesn't, that might well mean that there *are*! Nevertheless, the Professor slowly nudges the door open. Inside it's full of thick cobwebs, trailing across all the rusty handles and levers. The Professor enthusiastically starts to examine some of these levers, telling you that they were for moving the signals up and down. But you and Miss Crumble are much more interested in a large oak box in the corner. Unfortunately, however, it is locked . . .

Do you have either of the KEYS in the KNAPSACK CARD? If you do, place it exactly over the box's 'lock' below to see if it works – then follow the instruction. (You may try both KEYS if you have them.) If you don't have either of the KEYS – or your KEY doesn't work – go to 173 instead.

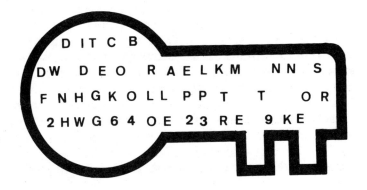

242

You now enter the tunnel, Spooks reluctantly trotting at your side. It grows darker and darker, more and more eerie. 'How long do you think it is, Professor?' you ask nervously over your shoulder. But the Professor doesn't answer. You and Miss Crumble turn round to find out why. He's not there! He must have absent-mindedly stopped somewhere farther back, perhaps to examine the tunnel wall. 'Professor Bones!' you and Miss Crumble both shout back down the tunnel. 'Professor Bones, where are you?' To your relief, he suddenly appears – but there's a loud wailing coming from behind him. Is it just echoes of your shouting, or is it something more sinister? You all anxiously peer into the darkness, wondering if a ghost is going to come out of it . . . **Go to 325.**

243

Your intrepid little group has walked a good couple of miles from the stone cross when you spot an eerie sight ahead. It's almost as eerie as that horrible iron bridge. 'What a gloomy-looking castle!' the Professor remarks as you stare through the mist at its black jagged outline. 'In fact,' he adds, 'I think it's the gloomiest-looking castle I've ever seen.' You quite agree with the Professor. If ever a castle was likely to be haunted, you would say that one was! But perhaps it could be of some use to you. If you could find it on the map, then it would show you roughly where you were . . .

Use the MAP to find which square the castle is in – then follow

the appropriate instruction. *If you don't have the MAP in the KNAPSACK CARD, you'll have to guess which instruction to follow.*

If you think B1   go to 8
If you think A1   go to 212
If you think B2   go to 39

244

You and Miss Crumble let out a huge sigh of relief. It's not a ghost coming from the tunnel, but a startled sheep! It must have wandered in there to shelter from the wind. Spooks seems even more relieved than you both, and he yaps at the sheep, chasing it right away from the tunnel. He might not be any good with ghosts, but sheep he can handle! As for Professor Bones, he has been quite oblivious to the whole affair. 'Do you know,' he says vaguely, finally raising his head from his knapsack, 'I don't believe we brought that map with us.' ***Go to 73.***

245

You all jump back in shock as the door suddenly swings open! 'It couldn't have been locked after all,' Miss Crumble remarks with relief. 'It must have just jammed in a sudden gust of wind, and unjammed in another!' But as you all step out of the church, you can tell that no one is really convinced by this explanation. Surely the wind isn't that strong! So you make your search of the graveyard as swift as possible, soon leaving the church. You haven't walked very far from it, however, when you hear an eerie moaning coming from that direction. Is it a ghost? Is this what shut and opened the church door? You all nervously turn your heads . . . **Go to 154.**

246

The Professor eagerly tugs the little door and peers inside the collection box. 'What a find!' he remarks as his head almost disappears into the hole. 'What a terrific find!' You and Miss Crumble look at each other with excitement. Is some of the gold hidden in there? 'Gold? No, I'm afraid there's no gold,' the Professor disappoints you as he straightens up again. He holds up an old Scottish coin. 'The terrific find was *this*,' he explains. 'The vicar must have overlooked it!' Miss Crumble is just about to tell the Professor off for building up your hopes when Spooks discovers something else. It's another of the hijackers' codebooks!

If you don't already have it there, put the CODEBOOK into the KNAPSACK CARD. Now go to 211.

247

You all hurry back along the railway line, Miss Crumble in a terrible state. 'Perhaps the ghost train came along when we stopped at that branch line,' she sobs, 'but it was only visible to Spooks. Perhaps he boarded it and is now being carted off goodness knows where!' All her distress is for nothing, though, for when you arrive back at where the line divides, you see that Spooks is still there, sniffing at the lever for changing the points. 'So that's why my little poppet stayed behind,' Miss Crumble remarks proudly as she starts to examine the lever herself. 'There's something that could be a coded message scratched along this handle.'

Use the CODEBOOK to find out what this message says by decoding the instruction below. If you don't have one, go to 158 instead.

248

You continue to search the inside of the station but then you wonder if the hijackers would have chosen somewhere a little less busy than the entrance hall to hide their gold. For the station was still in use then, of course. It was only *after* the terrible tragedy that the line was abandoned. So the hijackers would have wanted to be sure that the hiding-place was one that was still safe when the station was open again the next morning. They couldn't possibly risk one of the passengers or station staff finding it. 'Yes, that's a good point,' the Professor agrees, thoughtfully stroking his beard. 'A very good point indeed! Now, where would the *least* busy part of the station be? At the very end of one of the platforms, I would say.' That's exactly what you were all dreading, though – having to walk along the eerie, windswept platform! ***Go to 63.***

249

Since you don't have the means to decode the message, though, Miss Crumble squeezes her way through the gap at the side of the huge door and enters the shed. She just makes it, breathing in as much as she can! The rest of you have just followed her, gasping at the vast, dark interior, when you hear a loud creaking outside. 'It s-s-sounds like that turntable we p-p-passed,' the Professor stammers. 'You did notice it, didn't you? It was a section of track on a revolving base so the trains could be turned round.' Yes, you and Miss Crumble *did* notice the turntable. But you also noticed that it looked far too rusty ever to turn again. And, anyway, it could hardly turn by itself. Or could it? You all nervously turn back to the gap in the door and peep through . . . ***Go to 298.***

250

When you have recovered from this haunting, record it on the GHOST COUNTER. Now go to 39.

251

The Professor's relief soon disappears, however, when you notice a smaller door along one side of the engine shed. And this one clearly isn't locked, because it's flapping in the wind! He nervously steps through it and leads you all into the shed's vast dark interior. You can just see an old locomotive in there and a couple of long carriages. You're about to examine them more closely when you hear what sounds like someone whistling a tune outside the shed. Is this merely the wind, or is it the ghost of one of the mechanics who used to work in there? You all nervously peep back out of the door to check . . . **Go to 82.**

252

You now take your first look round the dilapidated cottage. You find that you are standing in a small living-room. There are a couple of chairs and a tiny oak table but both these are almost lost under thick white cobwebs. 'Well, there's clearly no gold hidden here,' you remark, 'unless it's under the floorboards, of course. But we haven't time to lift all of them up. Let's try the bedroom.' The bedroom is even smaller and it is quite clear that the farmer must have lived alone. Lifting the moth-eaten bedspread so you can peer underneath the bed, you notice a small chest hidden there. You all excitedly drag it out and try to open the lid, but it's firmly locked.

Do you have either of the KEYS in the KNAPSACK CARD? If you do, place it exactly over the chest's 'lock' below to see if it works – then follow the instruction. If you don't have either of the KEYS – or your KEY doesn't work – go to 120 instead.

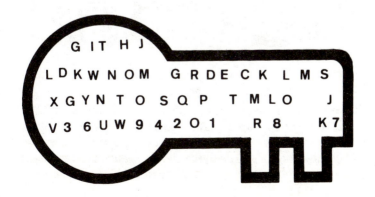

253

Miss Crumble needn't say a word to you as she raises her eyes apologetically from the special dice. It has obviously picked *you* to lead the way towards the eerie station. So you take the Professor's torch from him and nervously start to walk again along the track. You are soon entering the dark entrance hall of the station, the beam of the torch making spooky shadows all about you. It flickers over a rusty old luggage trolley in the corner and a woodworm-ridden bench. You all edge towards the cracked ticket window, finding a slim door at its side. This obviously leads into the ticket office. Wondering if the gold might be hidden in there, you try the handle. The door is firmly locked.

Do you have either of the KEYS in the KNAPSACK CARD? If you do, place it exactly over the door's 'lock' below to see if it works – then follow the instruction. (You may try both KEYS if you have them.) If you don't have either of the KEYS – or your KEY doesn't work – go to 227 instead.

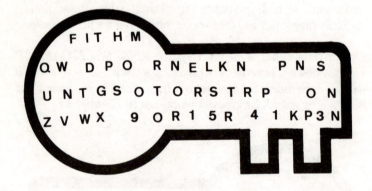

254

'It doesn't matter that we can't unlock the door, Professor,' Miss Crumble tells him with a secret wink at you. 'Look, the sliding window in the door is open a fraction. If you pull it right down, we can all crawl through it into the carriage – *you're* still going first, of course!' The Professor obviously wishes that Miss Crumble wasn't so observant but he keeps his annoyance to himself, and obediently tugs the sliding window. He's just opened it fully when a loud pounding noise suddenly starts above you, from somewhere near the shed roof. Is there a bad-tempered ghost up there? You all anxiously lift your heads . . . **Go to 80.**

255

Even though you're unable to decode the message on the door, the fact that it exists is still very good news. For who else was likely to have scribbled the symbols but the hijackers? Which proves that they did come as far as this after all. Much more eager about it, therefore, Miss Crumble now leads the way into the dark little hut. But her eagerness suddenly disappears again and she lets out a loud scream. She's sure she can see an old, bearded face in the far corner of the hut! As the Professor nervously points his torch in that direction you all wonder if this is a ghost . . . **Go to 60.**

256

When you have recovered from this haunting, record it on the GHOST COUNTER. Now go to 100.

257

Sitting down on one of the rotten pews inside the church, you all have a short rest. 'How strange, building a church in an area as remote as this,' the Professor remarks as he stares up at the sky through its collapsed roof. 'Perhaps there used to be more people inhabiting the glen in those days,' and then they were wiped out in a feud between clans. It was quite common in these parts. There was the terrible Glencoe massacre, for instance, when –' Before the Professor can give any of the grisly details, however, Miss Crumble suggests you now start searching the church. 'I'll ask my special dice for the best place to look,' she says, taking it from her pocket.

Throw the SPECIAL DICE – then turn to the appropriate number.

If ☠ thrown		go to 110
If 🦇 thrown		go to 295
If 👻 thrown		go to 45

258

'We're just going to have to think of some other way of trying to open it,' you remark as you all stare down at the locked chest, feeling very frustrated. 'If only we had a crowbar with us!' you add with a sigh. You're just giving the lid a really good tug, hoping that the lock is so rusty it can be forced open, when there's a very faint rumbling noise. You wonder where it's coming from, but then the Professor puts his ear to the railway line. 'There's a train coming!' he exclaims with horror. Is the ghost train about to make an appearance already? You all nervously stare back along the railway line, waiting for the train to emerge from the mist . . . **Go to 29.**

259

Miss Crumble utters not a word as she studies how her special dice fell but tensely leads the way through the carriage door. It was obviously *her* whom the dice chose! As you all follow her along the dark, musty carriage, you check the faded seats to left and right. You also check the luggage racks above them, but there's not a bar of gold in sight. Reaching the very end of the carriage, though, you find yourselves at a slim wooden door. There's a tiny semi-circular slot just above the handle, with the word 'vacant' showing through. It's obviously the washroom. 'Perhaps the gold is hidden in here!' Miss Crumble remarks excitedly. When she tries to turn the handle, however, she finds that the door is firmly locked!

Do you have either of the KEYS in the KNAPSACK CARD? If you do, place it exactly over the washroom door's 'lock' below to see if it works – then follow the instruction. (You may try both KEYS if you have them.) If you don't have either of the KEYS – or your KEY doesn't work – go to 141 instead.

260

'It's no use, Professor Bones,' you tell him as he continues to scratch his head at the message on the door. 'You'll never work it out without that codebook, I'm afraid. What a pity we didn't choose it as the item to borrow.' The Professor insists that with a bit more time, though, he might be able to work out the message even without a codebook. You know he's brilliant – but not that brilliant. You suspect that he's just trying to put off entering the gloomy cottage! Suddenly, though, he leaps through the door and you, Miss Crumble and Spooks follow in quickly behind him. You all lean back against it, pressing for all you are worth. You've just heard a strange wailing noise coming through the mist. Could it be a ghost? You all tensely creep up to the window to check . . . **Go to 208.**

261

You have to remind the Professor that you don't have the map with you, however. It was one of the other items that you borrowed from Mr Sporran. Your little group now starts to follow the farm track, noticing the complete absence of tyre marks along it. This shows that it obviously isn't used very much these days – if at all. But what's that humming noise coming from behind you? Is a tractor chugging along at this very moment, or is it some sort of ghost? You all anxiously look over your shoulders to check . . . **Go to 166.**

262

*When you have recovered from this haunting, record it on the **GHOST COUNTER**. (Don't forget: when you have recorded four hauntings, you must immediately stop the adventure and start the game all over again.) Now go to 129.*

263

But of course you didn't bring Mr Sporran's map with you! It's not that desperate, though, because it's soon quite obvious what the hut was for. Arriving there, you discover several rusty shovels and pickaxes inside. 'Ah!' exclaims Professor Bones, raising a knowledgeable finger. 'This is what's known as a gangers' hut. It was used by workmen who did repair jobs on the line. They would keep their tools here and use it for shelter if the weather turned . . .' But the Professor's voice suddenly trails off as you all hear a strange noise coming from outside the hut. It sounds just like a pickaxe being swung into the ground! Could this be the ghost of one of those workmen, you wonder, as you all nervously creep up to the window of the hut to check. No, surely not . . . ***Go to 202.***

264

Of course, without the codebook there's no way of telling if the message was written by a hijacker. 'Perhaps it was just scribbled by some child,' the Professor tries to console himself as he peers up at it. Well, Professor Bones might be a very brainy man, but he's certainly not a very logical one. How could a child possibly have reached right up there! Spooks is impatient to get moving and so you all start to follow him again. Your little group hasn't walked far from the monument, however, when a large hole starts to open up in the mist ahead of you. Is this quite a natural thing, caused by a gust of air, or is something suddenly going to appear there? You all dearly hope it's the first explanation . . . ***Go to 322.***

265

You quickly leave the eerie signal box and continue your trek along the railway line. Eventually, you reach a level-crossing. The old iron gates blow from side to side in the wind, clattering against the posts. A farm track crosses the railway line at this point and you wonder whether you ought to follow it for a while. This would seem an ideal unloading place for the hijackers. But just as you've decided to follow the track in a southerly direction the Professor notices several strange symbols scratched on the level-crossing gates. Could this be some sort of coded message?

Use your CODEBOOK CARD to find out what the message says by decoding the instruction below. If you don't have the CODEBOOK in the KNAPSACK CARD, go to 236 instead.

266

Since you don't have the right key to open the safe, you're just going to have to hope that the gold *isn't* in there. You all now start to make your way back towards the beginning of the tunnel. After a while, the Professor suddenly stops. 'I thought I felt something blowing on my head!' he exclaims, staring above him. 'It's a vent to allow the train's steam to escape. The wind sounds quite fierce up there!' But you begin to wonder if it *is* only the wind blowing through the vent. There seems to be a strange wailing sound up there as well. Is a ghost floating down through it? You all hurry right back to the entrance of the tunnel before turning round. 'Can you see anything?' the Professor asks, squinting through his glasses, as you all nervously peer into the darkness . . . ***Go to 70.***

267

You now start your return along the farm track, back towards the railway line. But as you walk away from the tunnel, you begin to worry that you didn't search it thoroughly enough. Perhaps you should have gone a little further down it and, who knows, the other end might have been nearer than you thought! 'That I very much doubt, dear child,' the Professor tells you with that knowing air of his. 'I would say that was an extremely *long* tunnel. There's a way we can find out as well. We can look for the spot where the tunnel emerges on Mr Sporran's map.'

Use the MAP to find which square the tunnel comes out of the hillside – then follow the appropriate instruction. If you don't have the MAP in the KNAPSACK CARD, you'll have to guess which instruction to follow.

> If you think E3   go to 40
> If you think D4   go to 283
> If you think E4   go to 10

268

You and Miss Crumble wait patiently for the Professor to discover that he doesn't have the map in his knapsack after all. But your wait becomes longer and longer – he still hasn't joined you inside the engine shed. 'I bet he's just trying to put it off as long as possible,' Miss Crumble whispers rather crossly as you both step outside again to go and fetch him. You find that the Professor is not searching through his knapsack at all, though. He's wildly staring back down the railway line, with absolute terror on his face! Wondering at the reason for this, you and Miss Crumble anxiously peer along the shadowy line yourselves . . . ***Go to 20.***

269

It doesn't really matter that you can't unlock the door because when you walk round to the back of the church you notice that there is another one. And this door is wide open, creaking backwards and forwards in the wind. You've all just squeezed into the crumbling building when you hear a shrill whistle in the distance. It's coming from the direction of the railway line! You all hurry back to the door and peer round it. Your wide, frightened eyes nervously scan the dark horizon . . . **Go to 220.**

270

Your little group now reaches the collapsed bridge. Spooks shivers as he stares up at the rusty girders way above him. Being a dog, he can't know anything about that dreadful incident, of course, but he certainly seems to *sense* something horrible about the bridge. 'Well, I think our best plan is to follow the railway line *back* from the bridge,' you suggest nervously as the loose girders continue to creak and groan all about you. 'But first, perhaps we should explore underneath the bridge itself, down that steep river-bank. Something might have dropped from the train just before it plunged to its doom. An important clue perhaps.' **Go to 320.**

271

You haven't followed the river very far when Miss Crumble suddenly spots a small chest lying on the rocky river-bed, about half a metre under the water. She instantly hoists up her skirt and wades in to investigate it. 'It's locked!' she calls back disappointedly to you and the Professor on the bank. 'It will need a key!'

Do you have either of the KEYS in the KNAPSACK CARD? If you do, place it exactly over the chest's 'lock' below to see if it works – then follow the instruction. (You may try both KEYS if you have them.) If you don't have a KEY – or your KEY doesn't work – go to 291 instead.

272
You're all just regretting that you chose not to borrow the codebook from the museum when the hose from the water tank suddenly makes a horrible creaking noise. Then it starts to swing slowly round as if it has suddenly come alive! Terrified, you all run away from it, only stopping when you're a good hundred metres further along the track. 'Oh, I'm sure it was just the wind that caused the hose arm to swing about,' the Professor remarks pompously (even though he had probably been the most frightened of you all!). 'If we look back at the tank,' he adds, 'I very much doubt that we'll see any ghosts.' As you very slowly turn your head, you only wish you could share the Professor's confidence . . . ***Go to 184.***

273
While you're all waiting for the Professor to come back down the ladder, Spooks starts to show interest in a small rock at the bottom of

the signal. He pushes it over with his nose, sniffing at something underneath. 'If that's a dirty old bone, Spooks,' his mistress warns him as he's about to pick it up in his teeth, 'you can jolly well leave it where it is!' But it's something quite different that the little dog carries towards her and drops into her hand. It's another copy of the hijackers' codebook. They also must have climbed the signal to get their bearings!

If you don't already have it there, put the CODEBOOK into the KNAPSACK CARD. Now go to 103.

274

When you have recovered from this haunting, record it on the GHOST COUNTER. Now go to 35.

275

You can just about make out that Miss Crumble is now entering the cottage. 'We really can't let her explore that spooky place on her own, Professor,' you remark, suddenly feeling rather guilty about it. 'I think we had better go and help her.' The Professor points out that Miss Crumble *isn't* alone – Spooks is with her. But you drag him along with you to the cottage and soon step through the dilapidated door yourselves. Far from your arrival reassuring Miss Crumble, though, it gives her the shock of her life. She hadn't heard you and the Professor come up behind her and when she suddenly sees you there she nearly jumps out of her skin! ***Go to 9.***

276

You all let out a huge sigh of relief as you now look over your shoulders at the wooden hut. It *was* just the wind that had caused the shutter to fly open. So you happily continue your walk along the railway line. The only one that doesn't look that happy is Spooks. 'What if it was a ghost in there!' the little dog seems to be thinking to himself, dragging his nose along the ground. 'I could have been only centimetres away from it while I was sniffing around for that gold. And did Mistress Crumble and those other two humans care? Not one bit! It's not me that wants the gold, anyway. I'd be just as happy with an old bone!' Well, maybe Spooks isn't thinking all these things. Who can tell with a dog? But his face certainly has a very sulky look! ***Go to 168.***

277

You've all walked quite a way from the needle of rock when you spot an eerie, jagged shape looming out of the mist ahead. It's a ruined castle. 'That would be a perfect place to hide the gold!' the Professor remarks, starting his odd little run towards it. 'Come on!' he urges the rest of you. 'Think of all those secret rooms and dungeons inside. It would be ideal!' You would rather not think of the dungeons, thank you very much, but you, Miss Crumble and Spooks chase after the Professor. On reaching the castle, however, you discover that there is an obstacle. 'And just how are we going to get that huge drawbridge down, Professor?' Miss Crumble asks. But Spooks trots round to the side of the castle and finds a small wooden door. What a find! Well, it would have been a find if it wasn't for the fact that the door was firmly locked!

Do you have either of the KEYS in the KNAPSACK CARD? If you do, place it exactly over the door's 'lock' below to see if it will open it – then follow the instruction. If you don't have either of the KEYS – or your KEY doesn't work – go to 300 instead.

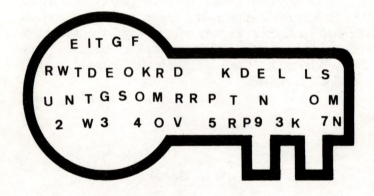

278

You all desperately give the door on the toolbox another tug, hoping that it will be so rusty it will just tear off. But your efforts are suddenly interrupted by a strange wailing noise coming from further down the tunnel. 'Oh, it's just the wind forcing its way through from the other end,' Miss Crumble says uncertainly. 'If it was a ghost,' she tries to reassure you, 'I would be getting one of my strange sensations!' Miss Crumble might not be getting a strange sensation, but you, the Professor and Spooks certainly are! You immediately hurry back to the tunnel entrance, dragging her with you. Only when you're safely outside do you anxiously turn your heads, peering back down the tunnel . . . ***Go to 292.***

279

You all now pass through the boathouse door, finding three very old rowing-boats inside. 'We'll search one each,' you suggest eagerly. 'These boats look like they date back quite a long way, even to the time of the train hijacking. So there's a chance the gold might be tucked inside one of them!' You all search the rowing-boats from bow to stern, feeling under the covered part at the front and under the seat, but there's not a bar of gold to be found. 'We should have guessed there wouldn't be,' you remark disappointedly as you now step outside again. 'Gold is too heavy to hide much of it in a boat. The boat could sink!' ***Go to 66.***

280

Your first haunting! When you have recovered from the shock, record it on the GHOST COUNTER. Now go to 193.

281

You now start to lead the others round the head of the loch, hoping that this will be the quickest way back to the railway line. 'Please go as quickly as you can, dear,' Miss Crumble nervously urges you from behind. 'I really don't like this misty, gloomy lake. I'm sure something horrible is about to jump out of it!' The Professor seems quite delighted by her admission. 'But I thought you didn't mind ghosts, Miss Crumble,' he points out. 'Indeed, I thought you actually went looking for them.' Miss Crumble is quick to cover up, however. 'Of course I don't mind ghosts, Professor,' she snaps at him. 'When I said something "horrible" I meant a monster in the lake. A harmless little ghost wouldn't bother me one bit!' ***Go to 100.***

282

'Ah, so it's me!' Miss Crumble exclaims, pretending she doesn't mind, as she studies her special dice. 'Well, off we go, then,' she adds heartily, marching straight into the tunnel. But the Professor calls her back. 'Just a minute, Miss Crumble,' he says, opening his knapsack. 'I'd like to find where this tunnel entrance is on Mr Sporran's map. It will show us exactly where we are.'

Use the MAP to find which square the farm track disappears into the mountain – then follow the appropriate instruction. If you don't have the MAP in the KNAPSACK CARD, you'll have to guess which instruction to follow.

If you think D3	go to 128
If you think D2	go to 105
If you think C2	go to 73

283

You finally reach the level-crossing again and you continue your trek along the derelict railway line. That little detour along the farm track and into the tunnel wasted a good hour. 'You won't find any bones buried *there*, Spooks!' Miss Crumble tells her little dog impatiently as he starts to sniff one of the rotting sleepers. 'Now do keep up or I'll have to put your lead on!' Trotting back to fetch him, however, she notices that there is something written on the sleeper which Spooks is sniffing. Has he found some sort of coded message?

Do you have the CODEBOOK in the KNAPSACK CARD? If you do, use it to find out what the message says by decoding the instruction below. If you don't, go to 102 instead.

284

'The message *must* have been carved by one of the hijackers,' the Professor exclaims gleefully after he has used the codebook to decipher it. He takes an excited breath before telling you what it works out as. It is this: *HERE IS TOO FAR AWAY FROM THE LINE – THE CHESTS HAVE ALL BEEN HIDDEN A LOT NEARER*. That information is really useful, except, of course, for the fact that you still have no idea where the railway line is! If only this mist would lift! But as you quietly stare around you, you get the impression that those grey eerie swirls *never* fully lift. ***Go to 39.***

285

All of you impatiently decode the message on the ladder and you come up with: *USE THIS TO REACH IT*. You look at each other with a cautious excitement. Does 'it' mean the gold? Did the hijackers hide the bars up in the roof somewhere? 'Don't forget,' you point out as you all quickly raise the ladder and prop it up against the side of the shed, 'the gold only had to remain out of sight until the hijackers came and collected it again. They probably intended that to be just a week or so later, so up in the roof would have seemed fairly safe to them. They just had to keep their fingers crossed that no repair jobs were done in that time.' You start to climb the ladder. Are you about to find the gold at last? ***Go to 228.***

286

When you have recovered from this haunting, record it on the GHOST COUNTER. Now go to 15.

287

Honestly! The Professor must have the shortest memory in the world. It was only back at that signal that he was reminded that you didn't bring the map! You now continue on your hike, but you haven't walked much further along the track when you think you hear the gushing of water. The sound's coming from the direction of that tank. Is it suddenly operating again? And if it is, what is it filling? Could it be the ghost train? Hoping that the gushing sound is just from a small brook nearby, you all nervously peer back up the line . . . **Go to 54.**

288

It's very tempting just to forget about the locked door and leave the eerie signal box. But it's a temptation you manage to resist. You notice how rotten the narrow door is and so you suggest to the others that you just try and force it open. You all push as hard as you can . . . and you're suddenly tumbling into the dark signal box! As you pick yourselves up from the floor, dusting off all the cobwebs, Miss Crumble suddenly screams. 'It's that broken window up there,' she gasps. 'I'm sure a face appeared briefly at it!' Hoping that Miss Crumble was mistaken, you and the Professor nervously peer towards the broken window yourselves . . . **Go to 6.**

289

'Who did it choose, Miss Crumble?' you ask as she studies her special dice to see how it fell. You enquire hopefully, 'Was it Professor Bones again?' But the solemn look she gives you makes it quite clear that the dice has chosen *you* to go first this time! So, playing fair, you carefully lead the little group down the embankment. The mist becomes thicker and thicker as you slowly approach the dark, fast-flowing river at the bottom. But your eerie detour proves in vain because there is no sign of the gold anywhere down the embankment. **Go to 161.**

290

Unfortunately, of course, you chose not to borrow the map from the museum. That's twice now that the map would have proved quite useful – maybe you decided on the wrong item. Anyway, you now start to follow the desolate railway line, all keeping very close together. You're afraid that at any moment the ghost train might come speeding towards you out of the gloomy mist ahead! Nervously listening out for its whistle, though, you suddenly hear a totally different sound. It's coming from behind you – and it sounds like *bagpipes*! 'Surely no one would be playing bagpipes in a place as remote as this,' you whisper tensely, 'at least not anyone human!' Could it be a *ghost* piper behind you? You all nervously turn your heads to find out . . . ***Go to 65.***

291

Miss Crumble lifts the chest out of the water, intending to bring it back to the bank so you can try and force it open. But you call to her not to bother. 'If you were able to lift it that easily, Miss Crumble,' you tell her, 'then it obviously contains something much lighter than gold. It's probably just fishing-tackle!' So she lets the chest drop to the river-bed again and carefully picks her way back to the bank. 'I bet it was cold in there,' you say but just as she's about to reply there's a loud swishing sound from further up the river. You all nervously turn your heads in that direction . . . ***Go to 238.***

292

When you have recovered from this haunting, record it on the GHOST COUNTER. Now go to 267.

293

You decide to visit the cottage so you can have a word with the crofter. He might be able to help you in your search for the gold. But as you get nearer to the little stone building, you realise it has long since been abandoned. The thatched roof is falling in and all the windows are broken. This makes you all a lot more nervous about approaching. Perhaps the cottage is full of ghosts! But perhaps it also hides the gold . . . and so it is important that you put aside your fears. Miss Crumble has an idea. 'One of us can investigate and then call the others if it's safe,' she suggests. 'I'll throw my special dice to decide who that one is to be!'

Throw the SPECIAL DICE – then turn to the appropriate number.

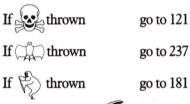

If ☠ thrown   go to 121

If 🦇 thrown   go to 237

If 👻 thrown   go to 181

294

You're all desperately trying to think of some way of opening the grit box without a key when Spooks lets out a terrified howl. To begin with, you think it's just the storm that's frightened him but then he frantically tugs at Miss Crumble's tweed skirt, making her look across at the opposite platform. You and the Professor do so as well, your eyes suddenly fixing on the long station name there. Before it had read DARKGLEN HALT – but now it reads DON'T DARE HALT and the black lettering has changed to red! 'It's obviously a warning to us!' Miss Crumble exclaims, petrified. 'It's telling us not to hang around here. We'd better leave the station at once!' And, just to be on the safe side, you decide to leave the railway line altogether and hurriedly make your way back to Coldhaggis!

So you've had to abandon your expedition. If you would like another attempt at finding the hijackers' gold, you must start the game again from the beginning. Try setting off with a different ITEM this time to see if it gives you more luck.

295

Miss Crumble's dice apparently recommends that you should climb up to the tiny choir-stall to look for the gold. So you all mount the crumbling stone steps at the side, although, as usual, you and the Professor are rather doubtful about the dice's instructions! You're even more doubtful when you reach the little balcony. It feels as if it's about to collapse at any moment! You're just about to advise that you make your way down again when Miss Crumble notices some symbols carved into the wooden handrail at the front. It looks like some sort of coded message!

Use the CODEBOOK to find out what this message says by decoding the instruction below. If you don't have one, go to 225 instead.

296

'Never mind that we can't unlock the padlock,' Miss Crumble says, suddenly having an idea. 'Look, there's quite a large hole in the door where it's rotted away. It's just about big enough for Spooks.' She then places Spooks in front of the hole, ordering him to crawl through and have a quick sniff round inside. It takes a while before he obeys the order but he eventually squeezes through. A few seconds later, though, he emerges again and darts for cover behind the nearest tree. 'What on earth did he see in there?' the Professor asks nervously as you all quickly retreat to the tree yourselves. But it looks as if he's about to find out . . . ***Go to 142.***

297

'I'm afraid we didn't borrow the map, Professor,' you answer him politely. 'If you remember, it was one of the other items.' You now ask them all to follow you as you start to walk round the head of the loch. You're hoping that this will be the quickest way back to the railway line. 'It's not exactly a very pretty stretch of water, is it?' the Professor remarks tensely as you walk along its misty shore. 'In fact, it's the eeriest I've ever seen!' It's just at this moment that a strange wailing wafts towards you from the middle of the loch. Is it a monster? Or is it something even worse – a ghost! You all anxiously peer through the mists swirling on the lake . . . ***Go to 256.***

When you have recovered from this haunting, record it on the GHOST COUNTER. Now go to 95.

299

Miss Crumble's special dice insists that you should all keep to the *main* part of the railway line. Quite how a little picture of a bat could convey that you're not sure, but neither you nor the Professor are going to argue with her! So you continue to follow the railway line, ignoring the part that branches off to the right. 'It probably just leads to an engine shed,' the Professor remarks as you walk. 'A remote area like this wouldn't need any more than one line.' It's then that you suddenly notice that Spooks isn't with you! *Go to 247.*

300

Spooks is not daunted by the absence of the right key, though. He trots even further round the castle's crumbling walls, leading you to a part that is so low you can quite simply climb over it. You tentatively start to explore the castle's interior, but, quite frankly,

there is very little that can be explored. If there *were* ever any dungeons or secret rooms, they're now just heaps of rubble! So you soon leave the castle, but you haven't gone far when Miss Crumble thinks she hears someone calling from the walls. Nervously, you all look back at the ruin, hoping that Miss Crumble was mistaken . . .
Go to 250.

301

Your nervous little group has followed the shadowy track for another half-mile or so when Miss Crumble spots a large iron tank on stilts. You all wonder what it is but as you get a little nearer you notice that there is a long thick hose coming out of it. 'Of course!' the Professor exclaims with fascination, wiping his spectacles so he can have a better look. 'It's a water tank. That hose was to feed the water into the trains.' When you all reach the tank and walk round it, the Professor suddenly notices that some strange symbols have been scratched on its side. They appear to be some sort of coded message!

Use the CODEBOOK to find out what this message says by decoding the instruction below. If you don't have the CODEBOOK in the KNAPSACK CARD, go to 272 instead.

302

When you have recovered from this haunting, record it on the GHOST COUNTER. Now go to 103.

303

'I *knew* we should have borrowed the codebook from Mr Sporran!' the Professor exclaims, tightening his bony fist. 'As it is,' he adds, giving that fist a frustrated little thump, 'there's simply no way of telling whether this message was left by one of the hijackers.' You and Miss Crumble exchange a hopeless shake of the head. Honestly, the Professor's forgetfulness! It was *he* who suggested that you should leave the codebook and borrow one of the other items from the museum! Your little group now starts moving again but you haven't left the boulder far behind when you hear a strange noise coming from that direction. It sounds like metal scraping on something hard. Was that coded message chiselled by a hijacker after all – *and is this his ghost adding some more symbols*? You all nervously turn your heads, desperately hoping for another explanation for the sound . . . ***Go to 148.***

304

When you have recovered from this haunting, record it on the GHOST COUNTER. Now go to 18.

305

Having flung open the lid of the chest, you all excitedly peer inside. But the only thing in there is an old map. 'There's still hope,' Miss Crumble says, not to be daunted. 'Perhaps the map has a cross marked on it to show where the gold is hidden!' But as hard as you all study the map, there's not a cross to be found. You turn over the faded sheet of paper. There's a message scribbled across the back. It reads: *HARD LUCK, SID AND GEORGE, I'VE DOUBLE-CROSSED YOU BOTH. THE GOLD AIN'T HERE. I'VE HIDDEN IT SOME OTHER PLACE ALONG THE LINE.* 'Sid and George must have been two of the hijackers,' you comment thoughtfully, 'and this message was written by another of them. That one's double-crossed us as well!' But at least you might be able to find use for the map.

If you don't already have it there, put the MAP into the KNAPSACK CARD. Now go to 283.

306

Miss Crumble asks the Professor to shine his torch on the dice so she can see more clearly how it fell. 'It's chosen you, Professor!' she announces, squinting down at it. He looks as if he wishes he hadn't helped her out with the torch after all! Nevertheless, he nervously leads into the little hut, but not before suggesting that you locate it on Mr Sporran's map.

Use the MAP to find which square the mountain-rescue hut is in – then follow the instruction. If you don't have the MAP, you'll have to guess which instruction to follow.

>   If you think D3   go to 26
>   If you think D4   go to 83
>   If you think E4   go to 109

307

You're just about to give up with the engine shed when the Professor notices a long wooden ladder, resting against the side of the shed. 'It should reach right up into the roof,' the Professor calculates, tugging at his beard in thought. 'That's probably what it was for. In case any repair jobs were needed up there.' As he flashes his torch along the top edge of the ladder, he suddenly comes to a stop. There seem to be some symbols chiselled into it!

Use the CODEBOOK to find out what this message says by

decoding the instruction below. If you don't have the CODE-BOOK in the KNAPSACK CARD, go to 25 instead.

308

Miss Crumble deciphers the coded message on the handrail as: *YOU'RE ON THE RIGHT TRACK, MATES! BUT YOU'VE STILL GOT TO WALK FURTHER IF YOU'RE GOING TO FIND THE GOLD. IT'S NOT NOWHERE IN THIS CHURCH!* You and the Professor are delighted by this useful piece of information but Miss Crumble does not seem so pleased. 'What appalling grammar!' she remarks disapprovingly. 'No wonder those hijackers turned to crime. They were never going to make a living out of a decent profession!' ***Go to 57.***

309

'It's chosen *me*!' Miss Crumble announces glumly as she studies her special dice. 'Not that I'm worried about meeting any ghosties, of course,' she adds quickly. 'No, I'm just worried about losing my footing and falling into the river at the bottom!' But Miss Crumble manages to lead the way down without a single mishap and spots an old iron chest right at the river's edge! ***Go to 3.***

310

When you have recovered from this haunting, record it on the GHOST COUNTER. Now go to 283.

311

Having warily pushed the door open, the Professor now leads you all inside the abandoned station. It's as quiet as a grave in there! The torch's beam cuts through the darkness, lighting up an old timetable on the wall, then moves to the cracked window of the ticket counter. 'What's that?' you whisper tensely as it falls on a slim, rusty box attached to the wall. 'Oh,' you suddenly realise, 'it's just an old chocolate machine!' At the mention of 'chocolate', Spooks trots up to the machine, panting eagerly beneath it. He wants you to put in a coin. But his mistress gives him a stern rebuke. 'We've come here to look for bars of *gold*; not mouldy chocolate!' she chides him. **Go to 248.**

312

You now decide to make your way back to the railway line . . . but this is easier said than done. For the mist has grown a lot thicker while you were exploring the cottage and you're no longer sure which direction the line is! 'Don't worry, everyone!' Miss Crumble reassures you with a confident look on her face. 'Spooks will find the way. We'll get him to retrace our scent!' But Spooks's nervousness must have affected his nose because he leads you to somewhere very different from the railway line. You find yourselves standing at the edge of a gloomy, narrow loch! ***Go to 231.***

313

What a shame you didn't bring Mr Sporran's map with you! But you're soon able to *guess* the purpose of the hut because, entering by the creaking door, you discover some old shovels and pickaxes inside. It was obviously used by the workmen who did repair jobs on the railway line. You're just searching behind the tools in case one of the chests of gold is hidden there when Spooks starts to let out a low growl, sounding more and more frightened! 'What is it, Spooks?' Miss Crumble asks anxiously. 'Can you pick up someone's scent outside the hut?' Hoping that it is just a rabbit he can smell, you all creep back to the door to check. You hold your breath as you nervously peep outside . . . ***Go to 202.***

314

Professor Bones reminds you that you didn't bring the map, however. 'Your memory's as bad as mine,' he chuckles shyly. 'But don't worry, dear child,' he adds, twiddling his bow-tie, 'it might mean that you'll become a brilliant professor when you grow up!' You're just thinking what a frightening prospect that is – having the same funny little habits as him – when you all hear a strange howling noise way above you. It sounds as if it's coming from that stone tower! Dreading what you might see there, you all slowly peer up at it . . . *Go to 48.*

315

When you have recovered from this haunting, record it on the GHOST COUNTER. Now go to 103.

316

You remind Miss Crumble that you didn't bring the map, however. 'Oh, so we didn't,' she says quietly and she now steps into the station, nervously shining the Professor's torch round. The beam can barely penetrate all the dust hanging in the air but it moves from an old luggage trolley . . . to a timetable peeling off the wall . . . to the cracked window of the ticket office. Suddenly Spooks starts to bark. 'He always barks like that when he hears a whistle,' Miss Crumble remarks with concern. 'You don't think it's the porter's whistle, do you!' she adds, nervously looking out of one of the windows. You're sure that Miss Crumble is worrying unnecessarily, though. *You* certainly can't hear a whistle, nor can the

Professor. 'But a dog can detect a whistle more easily than a human can,' Miss Crumble reminds you. So you both anxiously join her at the window and peer out at the dark platform . . . ***Go to 160.***

317

'What a pity we decided not to bring the map with us,' you tell the others as you now start to follow the railway line. 'All we would have had to do is locate that station on the map,' you explain, 'and then we would've known roughly how far we had to walk. As it is, we don't know whether it's three miles, or thirty miles . . .' Your voice trails off as you suddenly hear a horrible whining in the distance. 'It must be the Phantom Piper!' Miss Crumble cries, referring to one of the ghosts the museum curator had warned you about. Mr Sporran had told you how the ghost had been heard playing his bagpipes on the night of that terrible accident, and on stormy nights ever since! 'Oh, we're just letting our imaginations run away with us, Miss Crumble,' you desperately try to persuade her. 'It's probably a sheep-dog whining in the distance.' But what's that suddenly forming out of the mist ahead of you? Perhaps it is the Phantom Piper after all . . . ***Go to 65.***

318

'The special dice has chosen *you* as the person to lead us back to the railway line, Professor,' Miss Crumble tells him as she studies how it rolled. 'It obviously thinks you're the cleverest!' she adds, rather artfully, you think. But Miss Crumble's flattery seems to do the trick because the Professor suddenly becomes inspired. 'I reckon our best bet is to follow this small river that runs into the loch,' he says enthusiastically, immediately taking the lead, 'because I have this strong feeling that somewhere ahead it will flow directly under the railway line!' **Go to 271.**

319

The special dice picks Miss Crumble herself to lead the way into the forbidding engine shed. Clicking her fingers to bring Spooks as close to heel as possible, she nervously heads for the small gap at one end of the huge folding door. She's just about to squeeze through when she notices that several strange symbols have been drawn on the door, scratched deeply into the metal. 'It appears to be some sort of coded message!' she exclaims excitedly.

Use the CODEBOOK CARD to find out what this message says by decoding the instruction below. If you don't have the CODEBOOK, go to 249 instead.

320

The others agree that your idea of exploring underneath the bridge itself is a good one. But what you can't agree on is who is going to go *first* down the steep embankment. None of you relishes the prospect. You might find some hijackers' mangled skeletons down there! 'We'll just have to let my special dice choose someone,' Miss Crumble says, tossing it on to the ground.

Throw the SPECIAL DICE – then turn to the appropriate paragraph number.

If 💀 thrown	go to 235
If 🦇 thrown	go to 309
If 👻 thrown	go to 289

321

Your little group now leaves the signal box and ventures further along the deserted railway line. After another half-mile or so, you arrive at a level-crossing. The old iron gates sway eerily in the wind, clattering backwards and forwards across the line. 'I wonder if *here* is where the hijackers stopped the train to unload the gold?' you ask thoughtfully. 'This would seem a perfect place for it. All they had to do was carry the chests of gold along this farm track that crosses the line.' So you decide to follow the farm track for a short distance. But in which direction – to the north of the level-crossing or to the south? Seeing that Miss Crumble is about to suggest using her special dice, you quickly flip a coin! You're to head *south*. ***Go to 34.***

322

When you have recovered from this haunting, record it on the GHOST COUNTER. Now go to 243.

323

You at last reach the railway line. 'I was beginning to think we never would!' the Professor exclaims as you start to follow it again. 'How about you, Miss Crumble?' he asks. She enthusiastically nods her head, rattling her beads as she does so. 'Oh yes, I was quite confident,' she answers. 'I knew my special dice wouldn't let us down. Although it's often not obvious to begin with, it always makes the right decision.' You can't help noticing that Miss Crumble looks a little bashful as she says this, however. You wonder how confident she really was! *Go to 107.*

324

Of course, the Professor's idea isn't really that brilliant at all, because you don't have Mr Sporran's map with you. You can't believe how forgetful he is! Perhaps it's a good thing he's so forgetful, though.

You're sure that if he'd had a clear memory of your previous ghost exploration together – how terrifying it had been! – then he wouldn't be here with you now. You can just about make out that Miss Crumble is now tentatively entering the cottage and you decide it would be unfair to let her explore it alone. The Professor rather reluctantly agrees. So you both hurry towards the cottage yourselves, stepping through the dilapidated door just after her. No sooner are you inside then you think you spot something at the window. It immediately disappears before you can work out what it is. But then it starts to appear again, something white materialising out of the mist . . . ***Go to 124.***

325

When you have recovered from this haunting, record it on the GHOST COUNTER. Now go to 27.

326
The Professor suddenly realises that you decided not to bring the map with you, however. It was one of the *other* items that you borrowed from the museum. But it's fairly obvious that this *is* the

right bridge . . . and the Professor knows it! 'I suppose there can't be many ruined railway bridges in the area,' he admits reluctantly as he starts to lead you all towards it again. He abruptly stops, however. 'What is it, Professor Bones?' Miss Crumble asks with alarm. His trembling hand points to a faint yellow glow in the distance. 'It's the ghost train!' he exclaims weakly. 'It's appearing already!' His shaking fingers grapple in his pocket for the ghost counter. It looks like your first haunting! *Go to 176.*

327

It doesn't really matter that you can't unlock the door because it is perfectly easy to use one of the broken windows. You pick the window where there's hardly any glass left at all and carefully insert your hand to unlatch it. Crawling through, you find yourself in a tiny living-room. It smells badly of mould and there are cobwebs trailing all over the sparse furniture. You quickly pass through to what was obviously once the bedroom, the small wooden bed still there and covered with even more cobwebs. No ghosts so far! But then you suddenly hear tapping on the window-pane behind you. You nervously turn your head, hoping that it's just the Professor and Miss Crumble come to see how you're getting on . . . *Go to 274.*

328

You can wonder all you like, though. Since you chose not to bring the map with you, you'll never know whether the needle of rock is shown on it. As you all continue your hike through the mist, Miss

Crumble starts to complain about Mr Sporran at the museum. 'Why that silly hairy-knee'd man wouldn't let us borrow all of the items, I don't know!' she moans. 'It's not as if he's never going to see us again!' But Miss Crumble might have spoken a little too soon. For there's suddenly a flapping sound above you, then a piercing cry. Is this a ghost? you all wonder in terror . . . ***Go to 71.***

329

You're just nervously wondering if some evil force is *luring* Miss Crumble along the bridge, drawing her to her doom, when she suddenly stops. 'Don't worry, dear child,' she reassures you. 'I wasn't going to walk right over the edge. No, I risked coming all this way because of this small chest I'd spotted on the line.' You and the Professor had been so concerned about Miss Crumble's safety that neither of you had noticed the chest until now. So you both suddenly become very excited! Have you found some of the gold already? You all eagerly try to open the chest but you find that it is firmly locked. Would one of Mr Sporran's keys perhaps open it?

Do you have either of the KEYS in the KNAPSACK CARD? If you do, place it exactly over the chest's 'lock' below to see if it works – then follow the instruction. If you don't have either of the KEYS – or your KEY doesn't work – go to 258 instead.

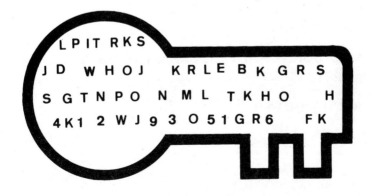

Other exciting titles in the Hodder and Stoughton Adventure Game Books series are:

FAMOUS FIVE ADVENTURE GAMES:

THE WRECKERS' TOWER GAME
THE HAUNTED RAILWAY GAME
THE WHISPERING ISLAND GAME
THE SINISTER LAKE GAME
THE WAILING LIGHTHOUSE GAME
THE SECRET AIRFIELD GAME
THE SHUDDERING MOUNTAIN GAME
THE MISSING SCIENTIST GAME

ASTERIX ADVENTURE GAMES:

ASTERIX TO THE RESCUE
OPERATION BRITAIN

THE PETER PAN ADVENTURE GAME:

PETER'S REVENGE

BIGGLES ADVENTURE GAMES:

THE SECRET NIGHT FLYER GAME
THE HIDDEN BLUEPRINTS GAME

THE FOOTBALL ADVENTURE GAME:

TACTICS!

GHOST ADVENTURE GAMES:

GHOSTLY TOWERS

WHO-DONE-IT ADVENTURE GAME:

SUSPECTS!

BATTLE QUEST:

CAVES OF FURY
TUNNELS OF FEAR